The Colors of My Past

Laura Esquivel

ISBN For this edition: **978-1-953596-00-0**

ISBN For eBook: **978-1-953596-01-7**

Library of Congress No. **2020917334**

The Publishing Portal
Los Angeles, CA
www.thepublishingportal.com
Printed in the United States of America

Cover Design by: **Jordi Castells**

Book formatting by: **Last Mile Publishing**

TABLE OF CONTENTS

CHAPTER 1

"It all began with the Christmas Rolls."

"How so?"

"Well, the onions are supposed to be *minced*."

"And?"

"And I diced them."

"Was that the reason your mother snapped at you?"

"Of course not! The size of the onion cubes was just her excuse for attacking me. My mistake could've been easily fixed, but she just went *on and on* about how I never listen to her, and how every time I break the rules in her kitchen it just proves that I don't care about…"

"But you were aware that the recipe calls for minced onion?"

"So? Are you taking her side now? I thought that as my therapist you were supposed to have my back. Like you don't already *know* my mother hates me. What's wrong with you?"

"I'm just trying to figure out the emotional responses that trigger your eating disorder."

"I don't have an eating disorder!"

"You don't? Hmm, you do realize that I specialize in compulsive eaters, right?"

"You know what? Fuck you."

Maria grabbed her purse and stormed out of the therapist's office, slamming the door behind her. She had to pause for a moment at the stairwell, so livid that she was out of breath. Maria made an effort to remember who had recommended this therapist so she could call them right away and give them a piece of her mind. What a stupid, insensitive hag this so-called therapist had turned out to be! How else was Maria expected to react after her husband's rejection and being shunned by her own family? Sure, she resorted to overeating when she was stressed out—which she thought was better than drinking or doing drugs—but that didn't mean she had a goddamn eating disorder. Bitch. Maria was done with her. The holiday season was stressful enough without having to deal with this woman.

Because of her seasonal affective disorder, Maria had to self-medicate just to be able to make it through her family's Holiday parties. The pills weren't always enough. Finding the right thing to wear was always a struggle. She planned her outfit around the clothes that could best way conceal her excessive weight, in anticipation of her cousins' sneaky, disapproving looks at her large midsection. Every now and then a random family member would ask—sometimes out of ignorance, sometimes out of spite—if she was pregnant. Maria always answered "yes". The following year, she expected the culprit to ask about her supposed child. They never did. This year, for the first time, she finally had something to surprise the extended family with, although she suspected that by now they knew all about the little scandal. In early December Maria had given birth to her first son, Horacio, a healthy, beautiful, but inexplicably black son. Jet black. As black as the new moon that marked his fate. As black as the dark Christmas that had befallen them.

Since the boy's birth, Maria's entire life had been turned upside-down. Her husband accused her of cheating. Her mother literally had a nervous breakdown. No one seemed to believe that

Chapter 1

the boy had been lovingly and legitimately conceived within the confines of her marriage.

Maria had been head over heels in love when she got married. She'd been looking forward to her child's arrival since the day she found out she was pregnant. She even went so far as to think that his December birth would help her overcome her aversion to the Holidays, but it just made everything worse. And the saddest part of the whole ordeal was that she couldn't even breastfeed the child. The emotional shock had too much of a negative impact on her body. Her hormones were out of control, and she went through a horrible post-partum depression. Despite that, every single day she tried her hardest to be a functional mother and to give Horacio her utmost loving attention and care, which wasn't particularly easy when it came time to feed a boy who refused to drink formula from a bottle and cried non-stop. Maria, exhausted, would break down and cry with him. When there were no more tears left in their eyes, when all they could do was sob, Maria and Horacio stared at one another, both of them pleading for under-standing. Maria would stroke the boy's curly hair and ask for his cooperation. Horacio—lacking the ability to answer—would stare back, and eventually surrender to the bottle.

When Horacio finally fell asleep, Maria would watch him for hours. The child was a mystery. There was no doubt he was hers; she'd seen him emerge from her body. His facial features perfectly matched the ones she'd seen on the ultrasounds. Maria found her-self longing for that profoundly innocent joy she'd felt the first time she heard her son's heartbeat when he was still a fetus. A heartbeat has no skin color; it's just a miraculous sound that an-nounces the beginning of a new life. When Horacio was inside her womb, everything was wonderful. Maria didn't have a single care in the world. She could never have imagined the chaos that would result from his birth. Carlos—her husband—had been present during the delivery, recording on his smartphone. Maria would never forget the look of absolute horror on Carlos' face when he saw the baby. He slowly put down his phone and looked at her. Maria thought something awful had happened, a stillbirth even. But Horacio wailed loudly, and Maria sighed with relief. Whatever could be wrong, then? Carlos and the Doctor exchanged a concerned look.

"What is it?" asked Maria.

As an answer, the doctor handed her the newborn.

Carlos left the delivery room before his wife could see him cry. Maria looked down at her baby and was shocked by what she saw. She held him with a heart full of love, but a head full of doubts. It's hard to believe how something as simple as skin color can elicit the strongest of reactions. Both Maria and Carlos were very light-skinned. Carlos even had blonde hair, and Maria had green eyes. Where could Horacio's dark skin tone have come from? As the days went by, her hunger for answers grew. The first solution she thought of was having a DNA test on both father and child, but Carlos refused. Then Maria considered hiring someone to trace their family trees, hoping of course that it was Carlos who'd had a black ancestor. On one hand she was scared to look further into it and open a Pandora's box, but on the other hand…she couldn't think of any other solution.

That afternoon, after her therapist's appointment, María was supposed to meet with an ancestry specialist. As she was leaving

Chapter 1

the office building where her therapist was located, her phone began to ring. It was her brother, Fernando.

"Where are you?" Fernando asked, a sense of urgency in his voice. Then again, Fernando had always been the nervous type.

"Leaving the therapist's…by the way, did you recommend her to me?"

"No…why?"

"Never mind."

"Listen," Fernando continued, "I'm calling to let you know that Mom just had a heart attack. We're on the way to the hospital. I left Horacio with Blanca. She says she'll babysit so you can come with me."

Maria was in shock. As long as she could remember, the holiday season had always been marked by some tragedy or another. How could anyone be expected to have joy in their hearts this time of year? What a nightmare!

Chapter 2

This definitely hadn't been her day. Horacio had cried all through the previous night. Carlos had grunted and protested several times, until in exasperation, he asked his wife if she could please make the child shut up, because he had to work early the next day. Maria tried her hardest, but she hadn't found a way to make their baby stop crying. She didn't know what time it was when both she and Horacio finally passed out from exhaustion. When she woke up, she was surprised to see Carlos gone. He had abandoned them, leaving only a letter in which he explained that he couldn't handle the situation, and that he needed space. He still loved her but he couldn't deal with Horacio. And to add insult to injury, Carlos left the DVD of Horacio's birth on the nightstand, like a john leaving cash behind for a prostitute. When she saw this, Maria felt a real, physical pain in the center of her chest, along with a terrible nausea that radiated from her solar plexus. But before she could truly process the loss of her husband, a piercing wail from Horacio demanded her attention. He was hungry. Maria picked him up and they cried in unison, even if for completely different reasons.

Later that morning Maria took the boy back to her brother's house so that her sister-in-law Blanca could watch him while she went to the hospital to check on her mom. Maria was supposed to relieve her sister Carolina, who had stayed up all night watching over their mother. She was running late, and traffic was awful. It was like the world was conspiring against her.

When Maria arrived at the hospital, she rushed to the elevator and pressed the button. The doors opened, and a nurse walked out. Maria walked in and as soon as the doors closed, she realized that the elevator was permeated with a terrible flatulent stink. Maria held her breath and looked through her purse for a handkerchief to cover her nose with, when the elevator doors opened once more and a very handsome doctor walked in. He noticed the smell too. Maria wanted to die. Through no fault of her own she was now presumably responsible for someone else's fart. And just her luck, the doctor was not only going to the same floor as her, but to the same room too. He turned out to be her mom's cardiologist. Before they stepped into the room, the doctor asked:

"Are you here to see Mrs. Alejandrez?"

"Yeah, but I didn't fart."

"Excuse me?"

"In the elevator. The smell was already there when I got in."

The doctor laughed out loud as he chivalrously held the door for Maria. They were met by a reproachful gaze from within the room. Carolina, Maria's sister, stared at them coldly as she held her mother's hand. Maria tried to wipe the smile from her face, and the doctor did the same.

"Okay mom, Maria's here. *Late*...but here." Carolina said without taking her eyes off her sister. "And look, Doctor Miller is here to check up on you as well, so I'm gonna head out. I have a *very* important business meeting. I'll be back this afternoon."

"Yes, my dear Caro. Thank you."

Carolina gathered her belongings in a huff and rushed out.

Doctor Miller picked up on the intense exchange between the two sisters and sensed how strained the room felt when Carolina spoke. It was also evident that Maria was terrible at hiding her feelings. He could tell that the woman was in pain, and not just because of her sister's rudeness or her mother's illness. He watched her take a deep breath and keep her lips shut tight so as not to argue with her sister in front of their sick mom. Then he noticed her turn and pretend to look out the window so she could discreetly wipe away her tears. So, when he was done checking on his patient, Doctor Miller asked Maria to step out into the hallway for a moment.

As soon as they were alone there, he placed a gentle, hand on her shoulder and asked:

"Are you okay? Do you want a prescription for anti-anxiety medication?"

Unable to take any more, Maria finally burst into sobs. The doctor gently held her in his arms, and Maria felt protected. A sincere hug—even from a stranger—was exactly what she needed at the moment. Doctor Miller stroked her hair, the way one might comfort a small child. Maria was profoundly grateful. She would never forget that act of kindness.

And sooner than expected, the doctor gave her another reason to be grateful. The next day, her mother passed away. Maria had to stay in the hospital to take care of all the paperwork. Carolina and Fernando had gone to the funeral parlor to make arrangements. Blanca was tasked with calling friends and family with the news, so she wasn't able to babysit Horacio. After a few hours of dealing with the hospital bureaucracy, Maria had to take a break. She was pacing the hospital hallway with her infant son in her arms, when she found herself in the presence of Doctor Miller once more. The cardiologist approached her and expressed his condolences with another hug. He then stroked Horacio's head and asked:

"Is this your son?"

"Yes", she answered timidly.

"Such a handsome boy."

Maria could sense that the doctor wasn't being superficially polite. He genuinely thought Horacio was a beautiful boy. It was the first time that someone had sincerely complimented her son since his birth, so Maria grinned with gratitude. Then she found it absurd to feel grateful just because someone else found her son beautiful. Maria expected everyone to see her child like Doctor Miller did, without prejudice. But she was nevertheless grateful and moved, so she swallowed hard and nodded her head in silence as she celebrated that someone else saw the value in what she loved most in the world. Maria felt less alone. Less rejected. And she wasn't being dramatic. Her close family, her so-called support structure, had not been supportive at all. On the contrary, when Maria went to the funeral parlor for her mother's wake the next day, her sister Carolina ran to meet her and stopped her at the door. She told Maria that her boss and other important people from work were paying their respects to their mother, and she didn't think it prudent for Maria to come in with Horacio, because the boy generated a lot of controversy and she wasn't emotionally fit to be giving explanations. "You piece of shit!" Maria thought, but instead of saying it out loud she scanned the room for her brother Fernando, who was walking towards them, sensing a confrontation. But as usual, he didn't dare speak up to defend Maria and put Carolina in her place. He had always been spineless.

Chapter 2

"Listen to me you bitch; I *will* walk in there. That corpse was my mother too, and I have just as much of a right as you to…"

"No, you don't," Carolina interrupted harshly. "Especially since mother died because you…"

"What the hell are you talking about? You mean because of my son?"

"Yes, exactly…that illegitimate…"

Maria handed Horacio to her brother Fernando with the intention of having her hands free to punch her sister, but before she had a chance to do so a powerful voice behind her spoke with great authority:

"What's happening here? Why are you making a scene?"

"Who are you?" Maria asked.

"Your grandmother", answered an elegant elderly lady. "And who is this boy?"

"He's my son…"

The lady then turned to Carolina, demanding in a harsh tone, "And what's your problem? Are you ashamed of your own nephew?"

"Grandma?" asked Carolina, incredulous. "Are you Grandma Lucia?"

"That's right. I'm the woman whom no one deemed important enough to be informed of her own daughter's passing. I had to find out through the obituaries."

"Grandma, I'm sorry…" began Carolina sheepishly. "I didn't know what to do…I don't know if Mom would've wanted you here…"

"And that's your excuse for not telling me about my own daughter's passing?" Lucía interrupted. She then addressed Maria, asking: "Is your sister as dense as she is racist?"

Maria's heart swelled with love for her grandmother. She hadn't seen her in many years and had forgotten her characteristically strong personality. Maria had always regretted that her mom had been estranged from Grandma Lucia for so long. She had to stop herself from kissing and hugging her grandmother.

"Listen here, girl," Lucia continued, pointing at Carolina. "If your sister and my great-grandson aren't welcome here, then I'm leaving with them."

Carolina shrugged.

Lucia approached Fernando and took Horacio from him. Carolina, fearing that Lucia and Maria might try to force their way into the funeral parlor, stood her ground in front of them. Fernando handed the baby over to his grandmother, while he quietly and timidly said:

"Hi Grandma, it's me, Fernando."

Lucia patted Fernando on the cheek but said nothing. It was past time for greetings. And contrary to Carolina's expectations, the matriarch turned on her heel and strode away regally.

"Let's go Maria! We don't need to be in a room full of vultures to pay our respects to the dead."

Maria obeyed without a word. Her grandmother had given her the best excuse to leave with dignity. As they walked away, Maria said:

"Thank you for this, Grandma, but you didn't have to leave too…"

Chapter 2

"Oh, but I did. In fact, your sister is right, I have no business coming where I'm not wanted. And it's true, you know. Your mother didn't want to see me. I kept wondering on my flight here why I even bothered coming. Now I understand…I'm here for you and your son."

It had been a cold and sad winter morning, but for an instant the clouds parted and the warm, radiant sun shone down on them. Maria felt like she was in a bizarre Broadway musical, as Cyndi Lauper's cover of "On the Sunny Side of the Street" blasted from the speakers of a nearby sandwich shop. Maria and Lucia exchanged a knowing look and smiled, despite the bitter altercation at the funeral parlor. Still smiling, they continued down the sunny side of the street, walking to the rhythm of the upbeat music that marked their spectacular exit.

Scan to listen to *On the Sunny Side of the Street*

Chapter 3

Maria decided that she really liked Grandma Lucia. On the flight to Piedras Negras, Maria witnessed the full extent of her grandmother's incredible warmth and integrity. Lucia had a striking personality. She was very good looking at eighty-one, strong, discreet, sincere, and kind. Although capable of raising her voice to demand what was rightfully hers, she also seemed at peace in the most profound silence. Lucia had not interrogated Maria like everyone else, nor had she hinted that she doubted Horacio's legitimacy. Maria was almost moved to tears by the tenderness with which Lucia held and kissed Horacio, and by the way the baby responded to her. As soon as his great-grandmother took him in her arms, Horacio fell into a deep, blissful slumber upon Lucia's large bosom. It was relaxing to see her child sleep so peacefully, and Maria finally felt a little bit of relief.

Maria had always felt anxious at airports and having a newborn in her arms made it worse. She was already overwhelmed by all the decisions she had to make in packing her bags and choosing a seat on the airplane. They weren't exactly complicated decisions, but Maria had so much to process that her mind struggled with them. She hated window seats, because if she needed to get up and use the restroom, she had to inconvenience the other passengers. And she didn't like the aisle seat either, because she couldn't stand the silent pressure from the passengers in her row once the plane had landed, all looking to disembark in a hurry like rats abandoning a sinking ship.

Fortunately, Grandma Lucia had been sent from the heavens to bring the help Maria so desperately needed. Feeling overwhelmed, but finally supported, Maria settled down in her airplane seat and tried to get some rest. Leaving everything behind to go live at Lucia's ranch for some time was the best decision she'd ever made. It meant she could be far, far away from the collapse of the world she and Carlos had built together. It meant not seeing her home torn apart piece by piece, not knowing which of their possessions Carlos would take with him or leave behind. Not seeing the flowers in her garden wilt. She was also not looking forward at all to the arguments with Carolina over mother's inheritance. Maria wanted nothing to do with her past. She deserved a moment to breathe, and since she was still technically on maternity leave, she could afford to do so.

Lucia's driver picked them up from the airport and drove them to the ranch, where all the employees were waiting to greet them. Chencha—a woman roughly grandma's age who was the housekeeper, and a direct descendant of another Chencha that had worked at the De la Garza ranch for years—led Maria to the room where she and Horacio would be staying. It was an ample yet cozy bedroom. There was a nightstand by the bed, a desk in the middle of the room, a vanity, and even a cradle with a mosquito net. Maria was surprised at how quickly the ranch staff had arranged to make everything ready for her, especially on such short notice. She also found several boxes of diapers, formula, and a baby bathtub. Absolutely everything had been thought of, and both Maria and her child's needs were completely covered.

As the days went by, Maria learned the reason for that organizational miracle: her grandmother kept an enormous warehouse that could rival that of any film production studio. Inside it she kept an inventory of all types of objects, including beds, pots, comforters, chairs, lamps, pillows, umbrellas, photo cameras, obsolete telephones, vinyl records, radios, slide projectors, film projectors for every possible format…almost anything one could think of. In short, a period film could be shot at Lucia's ranch without the need to rent any props. But even more amazingly, Maria learned that it was just as easy for Grandma to get rid of things as it was for her to acquire them. Lucia was by no means a hoarder. She had no qualms about throwing out superfluous, cheap trinkets; objects with no emotional significance. Like plastic bags, for example. Lucia was strongly opposed to them due to the ecological damage they cause, so they were practically banned from the ranch. Anyone who had to go shopping could choose from a magnificent array of jute, canvas, or paper bags to take with them. This position was in keeping with the general way of life at the ranch. Lucia funded the entire operation with the earnings from her business. She owned a factory that made bath soap, laundry detergent, and dishwasher liquid, as well as more specialized products to clean glass and to remove stains and grease. In the previous decades she had branched out, and now sold a line of body products that included shampoos, toothpaste, and lotion. Lucia's business was quite successful and allowed her a comfortable life.

Maria had only one complaint about life at the ranch: there was no way to get online! It was a disaster for someone as addicted to social media as she was.

"Wi-Fi? No, we don't have that here…" said her grandmother, when Lucia asked for the password. "What do you need to get online for?"

"Uh, so I can send and receive email, stay informed about what's happening in the world, and…"

"No darling, all you need right now is time for yourself…Everything that the world of technology apparently gives you, it really takes away from you."

"What do you mean?"

"Modern technology has a way of becoming your master, of enslaving and controlling you. It tells you what to do and when to do it, sets your rhythm, and leaves you no time for yourself. It keeps you preoccupied with things that don't really matter…what you really need is to recover your inner peace."

Maria begrudgingly accepted that her Grandmother was right, and kept her mouth shut. She knew full well that nothing good could come of her trying to see what Carlos had been up to on Facebook. Or from reading her friends' comments about their breakup, or from keeping tabs on the number of violent deaths in the country in the last few hours. Instead she silently drank the oatstraw tea that her grandmother made her, which was supposed to help her relax. Maria drank it as a courtesy but had no illusions about its supposed calming effects. If the anti-anxiety medication Dr. Miller had given her wasn't doing anything, what could a simple tea do? She was, of course, underestimating her grandmother's profound mastery of herbal medicine. The tea not only calmed her nerves, it also made her so relaxed that she forgot about trying to get online. After feeding Horacio his formula and putting him down for the night in his crib, Maria hit the mattress and passed out.

It was 8 AM the next morning when she woke up to the sound of the ranch dogs barking. Maria sat up with a jolt. The sun was out, and her son hadn't cried once throughout the night! She ran to the crib and found that the child was missing, then rushed out into the hallway and heard the faint sound of singing coming from the kitchen. She opened the door and found Horacio in Lucia's arms, sleeping like a log while his great-grandmother sang him a lullaby in the Náhuatl language. When Lucia looked up and saw her granddaughter, she grinned and asked:

"Good morning! Did you sleep well?"

"Yes Grandma…I just woke up" … said Maria groggily. "It's really late, huh?"

"Well, that depends. Time is relative. But don't worry, what's important is that you recovered some strength. You really needed to rest."

"Has Horacio been sleeping this whole time?"

"No, he began to cry at about four in the morning. You didn't seem to hear him, so I took him from the room to let you sleep…"

"I'm so sorry Grandma, it won't happen again…"

"Oh, it's no bother at all. I'm usually up by then and caring for your child is the best gift I've received in a very long time."

"Did he drink his formula?"

"Yes, without a fuss. At first, he tried to put up a fight, but I mixed a bit of wheat sprout *atole* into the bottle, and—although I think he found the taste strange at first—he drank it all. Look how peaceful he is now."

"But Grandma, why did you give him *atole*? Won't it make him sick?"

Lucia laughed, clearly amused. She handed the baby back to Maria and proceeded to give her granddaughter a full lecture on the nutritional properties of sprouts while she prepared breakfast for the both of them. First, she grabbed an old cast-iron *comal* and put it on the fire. Then she took some balls of flour dough from the refrigerator and began to flatten them on the kitchen counter with a rolling pin. The rhythm of her flattening was impeccable. Each ball of dough was soon transformed into a perfectly round tortilla. The contact between the rolling pin and the dough, and between the dough and the table created a hypnotic beat, and Lucia moved about the kitchen like a ballerina on a stage. Maria had seen her mother knead tortillas many times, but never the way her grandmother was doing now. Her mom had a rigid technique, while grandma Lucia applied a certain degree of sensuality to every motion.

After the tortillas had been pressed, Lucia placed them on her old, trusty *comal*. Nothing ever stuck to it, because it was used exclusively for flour tortillas. Through the years it had developed a protective coating a thousand times more effective than teflon or any non-stick surface advertised on television. The secret was that the *comal* was never washed. After it had been used, Lucia wiped it down with a paper towel. Maria was enthralled by the sight of her grandmother laying the raw tortilla on the *comal* as part of the cooking ritual which consisted of three steps: placing the tortilla and waiting a few seconds until a few bubbles formed on the surface, then turning it around and waiting for it to balloon. Then finally, flipping the tortilla once more so the side that had received less heat could turn golden brown. While she tended to the tortillas, Lucia chopped some onion and fried it in a different cast-iron pan. It was also big and beautiful, and no food stuck to it either because it had been treated the same way as the *comal*. Once the onion was sautéed, she added chopped tomato and chile, and then a few eggs that had been harvested from the chicken coop that morning. While the eggs cooked, she heated up some beans and turned on the coffee machine. In the middle of all of this, Lucia didn't miss a beat on her lecture about the benefits of sprouts, complete with accurate technical terms. This herbal lesson combined with the delicious breakfast proved to Maria exactly why her grandmother had earned a PhD in Chemistry and was considered the best cook in the region. As she listened, Maria remembered hearing once that Lucia had been the first woman to study chemistry in the state of Coahuila. Maria's mom, despite never talking about Grandma Lucia, had once mentioned it with pride, but then had quickly corrected course and said it was a pity that her mother had wasted her higher education when she chose to devote herself to healing plants and herbs. Maria never understood why that was a bad thing and was amazed by her Grandmother's extensive knowledge. She knew exactly what she was doing when she gave Horacio the wheat sprout *atole*. But what impressed Maria the most was observing Lucia as she moved about the kitchen like an alchemist. Her grandmother was definitely a master of rhythm, time, quantities, and potions. The warmth from the kitchen—in stark contrast to the cold outdoors— along with the aromas, and the calm breathing of Horacio as he slept in her arms, made Maria feel like part of a family, something she hadn't experienced in a long time. She felt like a small girl, engulfed and nurtured by kindness and love.

Suddenly, a memory that had been long hidden began to bloom inside her mind. The process had been set in motion the moment she set foot in her grandmother's house. Maria immediately recognized the smell of the old furniture. It was a peculiar scent that over the years had settled into every couch, curtain, rug, and bed; the smell of a home in which something had been cooked every day. That morning, the smell of the Christmas tree Lucia had put in the living room—along with the delicious smell from the kitchen—had triggered Maria's recollection of a Christmas dinner many years ago. Memories, sounds, echoes of color, and emotions that had all been festering under the surface of Maria's memory came back at the speed of light. She tried to think that everything might be okay, that she would be able to emerge un-scathed from this plunge into her childhood memories, but she failed to account for the way one thought leads to the next, like the successive ties in a railroad track, arranged one after another so the locomotive can glide over them on its determined path. Once in motion, there's no turning back. Jumping off a moving train is dangerous, especially if it's running at full speed. This put Maria on a collision course with her destiny, because Lucia—in an attempt to delight her granddaughter's palate—was heating some Christmas rolls in the oven. The rolls had been prepared for Christmas Eve, and these were leftovers. Maria was grateful for Lucia's culinary attentions, but as she gave the first bite, she not only recognized her grandmother's expert seasoning, but also col-lided head on with a hidden memory. And it was a particularly painful one.

She was just a small child, eating a Christmas Roll by the foot of the Christmas tree, when she heard yelling from the kitchen. Her mom and grandma were arguing at the top of their lungs. And then her mom burst out of the kitchen furiously, snatched the roll from Maria's hand and threw it on the floor, then dragged the girl out of Lucia's house by the arm, slamming the door loudly behind them.

Without stopping to think twice, Maria asked:

"Why did my mom get mad at you one Christmas when I was little?"

"Because your brother and sister wanted to open their presents before midnight, and I gave them permission to. Your mom was very upset, because she said we were breaking the rules of Christmas…"

"*That* was her reason for never coming back? For never wanting to see you again?"

"No, that was the excuse she found to vent her anger. The real reason was something else…"

"What was the reason, then?"

"That I cheated on your grandfather," Lucia said without skipping a beat or changing her matter-of-fact tone.

"What?"

"And when someone refuses to forgive you, all you can do is forgive yourself. It's not easy… but if you really want to know, I'll tell you everything, just not today. Now we should eat, or the food will get cold."

Maria considered herself a blunt person, but she had nothing on her grandmother. Lucia had just blurted out her terrible sin like it was nothing. The way one might say "it's cold out" or "it may snow later". Maria was dumbstruck, so she ate her delicious eggs a la Mexicana with some flour tortillas and a Christmas Roll, in silence. While she ate, Maria thought of Proust and his madeleines, of how the past is intimately intertwined with smell and taste. One small bite of a harmless Christmas Roll had been enough to sweep Maria away with an uncanny force into a torrent of data, memory, and information. As Maria chewed on the roll, Chencha made her grand entrance into the kitchen, hauling an antique cradle. It was likely from the second half of the 20th century and had been brought from the huge warehouse known around the ranch as the "trinkets and knickknacks room," to place Horacio in when he spent time with them in the kitchen.

"I found it, Lucia!" said Chencha.

"And just in time, we're about to have breakfast."

"Good morning Miss Maria. How are you this morning?" Chencha asked.

"Good. We slept great, actually."

"That's nice. Now, put your baby in here so you can eat in peace. It used to be your mother's, I believe…" said Chencha, as she placed the cradle on the floor next to Maria.

"It was," Lucia confirmed.

Chencha spoke quickly and abundantly. Her seemingly endless stream of words fanned the fire that fueled Maria's memory train. Maria placed Horacio in the cradle so she could eat comfortably, while Chencha babbled on and on. She talked for the sake of talking; from things as general as the weather to things as specific as the scuffle between the ranch dogs and a pack of wild dogs earlier that morning. Then she explained at length how the water in a small pond was freezing over, and suddenly —and without warning—jumped to a subject that made Maria's heart race.

"…and the whole staff wants to meet your great-grandchild, but I told them that the boy had to rest. They all just want to see with their own eyes what I told them, that Horacio is the spitting image of his grandfather, and…well, of his great-grandfather too. He got his eyes from the first, and the skin color from the latter…"

Maria almost choked. She turned to Lucia, who only nodded. Her train was about to derail! She was about to get confirmation that she was the one who had African ancestors, not Carlos. Not that she saw this as anything remotely bad, or even questionable. She'd never been a racist, much less now that she had this wonderful black son whom she loved with all her soul and believed to be the most beautiful boy in the world. The problem was that this information made her guilty in her husband's eyes, if not through infidelity, then through genetics. He was not as clear about his own prejudices.

Maria's expression, as usual, gave away the thoughts that ran through her head. Lucia immediately understood that her granddaughter was worried about the situation with her estranged husband, and fought to hold back the hint of a smile. It wasn't prudent to be so transparent about how proud she was to have a black great-grandchild, in light of the uproar the baby's birth had caused. But for Lucia, Horacio represented the culmination of her deepest hopes. She remembered that when she was pregnant with her daughter Luz Maria, she made a bet with her husband Felipe on whether the baby would be dark-skinned or not. And to Lucia's great disappointment, their daughter did not take after her husband's family. Felipe tried to convince Lucia that it was for the best, that it would mean their daughter would never be discriminated against, would not suffer segregation, exclusion or disdain. Lucia knew that Felipe spoke from his own experience, but her husband didn't understand just how proud Lucia would be to have a black daughter. It would have been the best way for her to show the world the beauty of a powerful and sensual race. It would also be a silent projection of her most sublime discourse, by way of materializing within a body the infinity of whispers that quietly proclaimed: black is beautiful! For nine months she entertained the hope that everything that she deeply loved would live on in her daughter: Felipe's full lips, his magnificent backside, his straight, neat teeth, his beautiful eyes, his unmistakable voice, his rhythm. She'd always been amazed by Felipe's dancing skills. He only had to move one muscle, just one, to light her on fire. His body oozed raw sexuality. Lucia never met anyone who could dance better than her husband, which made it especially tragic when he became a paraplegic. They could never dance again, or make love the way they used to, although they certainly found ways to express their intense love by kissing, caressing, and gazing silently into each other's eyes.

Now, as Lucia admired Horacio's good looks, she couldn't help but enjoy the paradox of life. Destiny did not give her a black daughter, but it did give her a black great-grandchild. A child of immeasurable beauty that no one expected, who had surprised everyone upon arrival. Lucia found a hilarious irony in the fact that her daughter Luz Maria, who'd been so proud of her chestnut hair and blue eyes and had tried so hard to hide her black heritage, had been unable to stop Lucia's deeply rooted desire from manifesting in her progeny.

The silence would have been absolute, if not for the sound made by the pages of Lucia's old photo album as Maria flipped through them one by one.

Images are definitely silent. But although they have no voice, they tell the story of our past without the need for words. Through mute smiles.

Maria anxiously awaited the photo that would bring the truth to light. Page after page, she imagined a carnival barker shouting: "Step right up, ladies and gentlemen, and witness something never seen before!" A secret was about to be revealed, and her palms were as sweaty as the roof of the ranch house. The sun was shining, and it had thawed the frost from the previous night. Each droplet that fell to the ground made a peculiar sound, not unlike a drum-roll that anticipated the grand moment of revelation.

Maria and her grandmother were sitting on the floor of Lucía's bedroom. Beside them, Lucia's trunk full of memories and mementos sat wide open. Lucia reached in and pulled out more photographs to show her granddaughter. It was an intensely beautiful, intimate, and magical ritual. Maria had to control her urge to rush through the pictures just to find the one she was most interested in.

She found one of the photos especially striking. It was a beautiful woman on a horse, proudly sporting a pair of crisscrossed cartridge belts on her chest.

"Who's this?" Maria asked, lightly tracing the cartridge belts with her index finger.

"That's Gertrudis, my great-aunt."

"Did she fight in the Revolution?"

"She did."

"And who is that standing beside her?"

"Her husband Juan. He was also a general of the Revolution."

"And this?"

"Their son, also named Juan. Juan Felipe actually, but he went by Felipe."

Maria carefully examined a celluloid medallion that contained an oval-shaped photograph framed in a flowery pattern. It was of a strikingly attractive, light-eyed, mixed-race man.

"What a handsome guy!"

"Yes, my father-in-law was very good looking."

"Your father-in-law? I'm talking about the man in this picture."

"Oh, right. Sorry. You've probably been kept in the dark about our family history. I married Felipe, Aunt Gertrudis' grandson...The son of the son that she had with Juan Alejandrez: Juan Felipe, the man in this picture. And before you ask: yes, I married my second cousin."

"And he was part black?"

"Yes."

"Is that why my son is black?"

"Yes, and because your grandfather's mom, Loretta, was also black."

Maria was mesmerized by the photo of her great-grandfather, especially by the uncanny resemblance between him and her son. They both shared the same striking blue eyes. After observing the similarities for a while, Maria broke the silence and asked:

"Did my mom ever see these pictures?"

"Of course, she did."

"Then why didn't she say something when Horacio was born? Why did she keep quiet?"

"Because it was painful for her to speak of her past. If she mentioned your grandfather, she would've had to mention me, and you remember how much she disliked me." Lucia said with a hint of sadness.

"But how could she do this to me? I was being shunned by everyone, for god's sakes! My marriage was ruined!" Maria continued, while taking pictures of the photographs with her smartphone. She planned on sending them to Carolina along with a kind message that would probably say something along the lines of "Look bitch, this is why my son is dark-skinned. Because of OUR GRANDFATHER." Oh, and Carlos would get one too, saying "proof that I didn't cheat on you." It was a shame that she couldn't send either message because, of course, there was no Wi-Fi. To vent her frustration, Maria retreated to her bedroom and tried to draw up a family tree with the information she had.

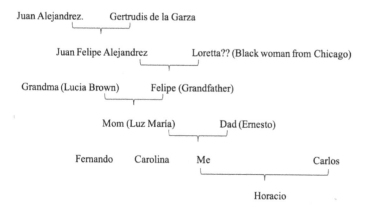

Chapter 4

Lucia took a slow drag from her cigarette. Digging up old photographs with Maria had also stirred something deep inside her, so she'd decided to go out to the porch to quell her memories and force them to retreat to the depths of her subconscious, where they could do no harm.

The ranch was completely silent. Everything was still. The quiet of the winter afternoon was the perfect environment for keeping her eyes shut and thinking of Felipe without distractions. Lucia was well aware that every time she thought of Felipe it was a risk. She feared that a turbulent memory might steer her to the dark part of her mind, to the things she ardently tried to hide. But she forgot about those silent mental constructs that don't announce their arrival. Those quiet, dark thoughts that are especially devastating when they catch you off-guard. A single thought is enough to tear one's entire world down, along with the set design, curtains, masks, and wardrobe. And from the ruins, the dead and the ghosts rise, bringing back with them everything that had been buried, that had been hiding behind a sarcastic, guilt-soaked smile. That afternoon, Lucia learned that keeping her mouth shut was not enough to silence secrets. She'd forgotten that scents cannot be silenced; they are loud, they break through barriers and rise to the surface at the first opportunity. A faint lavender aroma from her garden forced her to remember the smell of Felipe's freshly shaved face. Lucia used to help her husband shave, because his facial hair was very thick. The pleasant lavender scent was immediately followed by the pungent smell of fresh blood, reminding Lucia that she was alone, but not safe.

Maria had gone into town in search of a coffee shop where she could get internet access. As soon as she was able to get online, Maria uploaded her ancestors' pictures to Facebook, tagged every single one of her living relatives, and proceeded to devour an enormous a slice of chocolate cake as she waited for the reactions to start coming in. It didn't take long. Carolina—scandalized by the pictures of her supposed grandfather and great-grandfather—immediately fired off a private message to Maria, in which she implored her to stop lying. "You're hurting the family by making up all of these stories! I don't know and I don't care where you got those pictures of Africans but they have nothing to do with us!" The message ended with a firm demand to remove the pictures and stop tormenting their relatives. Maria was incensed by the message, so she called her grandmother to let her know that she'd be out longer, exchanging belligerent emails with her sister. Fortunately, Lucia had taken the right precautions; considering that Maria wasn't fit to drive in her current emotional state, she'd sent her granddaughter into town with the driver and with Chencha—who could look after Horacio while Maria let loose the dogs of war. Lucia understood the source of Maria's fury. She herself was no stranger to scorn—from family, friends, and strangers—having married a mixed-race man who was also her second cousin. Although in her time there was no Internet, aggression and hatred still found a way to "go viral." In the end the result was still the same; it brought suffering, one way or another.

Chapter 4

Lucia remembered the disapproving looks she got the first time she danced with her cousin. Felipe had just arrived in Mexico from Chicago, and everything about him was immensely attractive to Lucia. The crowd whispered and murmured. In hushed voices, people commented that he must be the grandson of Gertrudis, the Revolutionary General. If anyone's memory failed, others only had to mention that Gertrudis was the one who ran off naked on horseback, and they would know exactly who she was. Sadly, Gertrudis' great contribution to the armed uprising that forever changed the social and political life of Mexico was overshadowed by the iconic image of a nude woman galloping off on a horse, which had become her legacy in the collective imagination. Her achievements on the battlefield and in social activism had been minimized with the passing of the years, because once the Revolution was over Gertrudis was so disappointed that the Mexican Constitution of 1917 didn't give the women the right to vote, that she left Mexico for Chicago in a fit of rage to join the women's suffrage movement in the United States. Upon her arrival she discovered that the politics of women's suffrage in that country were very complicated. One of the main suffrage clubs only fought for the right of white women to vote. When she learned this, Gertrudis sought out Ida B. Wells, a black woman who had founded the Alpha Suffrage Club of Chicago in 1913, and she joined her struggle.

Gertrudis' incredible luck led her to the Hull House neighborhood, where—unlike other immigrant communities—several ethnic groups coexisted in relative peace. Mexicans, Italians, Greeks, Poles, and African Americans lived in mutual respect, and a relative state of non-discrimination. That was where Gertrudis accomplished her greatest wish, that her son might grow up in a place where he wasn't known as the "mulatto" of the town. Nevertheless, many years later she couldn't stop her grandson Felipe from returning to Mexico, where his skin color—and his courtship of and marriage to his cousin Lucia—would once again become the talk of the town.

Lucia took an old, wrinkled, yellowish letter from the pocket of her apron. She had hidden it there when she was showing Maria the family pictures. It was a letter she'd written to Felipe, and she didn't want her granddaughter to see it.

"My love, do you remember when you had a body and we could hold one another? Your embrace bore the weight of the heavens. It was like lying under the shade of an ancient tree. It was a peaceful, quiet slumber. It was the certainty that nothing could ever hurt me. Do you remember when you had a mouth and we kissed each other like crazy? Do you remember how we loved each other after every kiss? Do you remember how, during one of our unforgettable nights of passion we calculated how many times we would make love in our lifetime? I seem to recall that our most conservative projection—considering we were almost 40—was that we still had 35,000 nights of love to look forward to. You died 4,535 days after that night, and we'd only reached a count of 9,075. That means you still owe me 25,925 nights of love. Today, at the beach, I wrote your name on the sand and the tide erased it. I understood that nothing can contain you now; you are no longer a body. You have gone home. Now you are a part of the ocean, of the wind, of the entire universe. I remember that night we spent in the desert gazing up at a stunning blanket of stars, when we began to talk about the Big Bang. You explained to me that our bodies are made of star-matter and that we have existed since the beginning of creation. From the very first celestial explosion. Your ashes will one day soar with the force of that blast. They are ignited with love. You, all of you, you are incandescent love. Love that doesn't die. Love that comforts. Love that remains. Love that doesn't hurt, no matter how much I cry."

When she finished reading the letter for the final time, she lit it on fire with the tip of her cigarette. No one would ever see it again. It was way too intimate, too painful. Lucia thought of how convenient it would be if we could just burn away our guilt. Her burden was so big, so overwhelming, that it forced her to do what everyone does when faced with such a situation: project the guilt on someone else. It didn't matter who, as long as it wasn't herself.

Her initial coping mechanism was always to blame Felipe, the man who died in her arms, who accepted defeat. She remembered his eyes, his skin, his voice! It was such a shame that despite his amazing voice, he never became an internationally acclaimed singer. When Felipe sang in a familiar and intimate environment for friends and family, he was captivating. But if he had to sing in front of a large audience, his throat would physically clamp shut. He was never able to get over his crippling stage fright. Nothing helped; not Lucia's support, not his own personal ambition. He didn't get over it. He never could.

Felipe's debilitating problem had first manifested at a Catholic Church near the neighborhood where he grew up. A neighbor of theirs had heard the young Felipe's melodious voice, and asked his mother Loretta if she would let him sing the Ave Maria at her upcoming wedding. Loretta agreed. Felipe even learned the lyrics by heart, having never heard the song before at the protestant church his family attended. The day of the wedding, Felipe began the song with his incredible voice and captured the attention of all the attendants. But when they craned their necks to see where the angelic voice was coming from, and Felipe felt everyone's eyes on him, his throat shut down and he was unable to continue. It was an absolute disaster.

Lucia cursed herself for having pushed him so hard to perform in front of an audience. Maybe it would have been better if she'd let him enjoy simply singing for his family. She felt a pang of guilt and shifted her thoughts to the damages that slavery can cause, not just to the individual who is owned by another, but to their descendants as well. Felipe was a man who carried the weight of all the world's fears on his shoulders. All of them. And they manifested in his throat. Slavery, then, was to blame for much of what had happened to him. It was the root of all his troubles, a constant reminder of pain, a rope around his throat, the paralysis of his vocal cords. Lucia tried to remember Felipe's voice: a thunderous, painful, sensual voice that could bring her to tears. The key to Felipe's short-lived success—obtained in spite of his anxiety to perform—was his phrasing. It was something of a mix between Frank Sinatra and Billie Holiday, yet completely unique, and not unlike a breathy prayer whispered in your ear. When Felipe opened his mouth to sing, he channeled the vibration of every wail heard on every slave ship that had ever crossed the Atlantic, of every scream held back by a black man or woman who had ever been lashed. Sometimes his songs felt ritualistic, like the spirituals sung by slaves under the moonlight.

Chapter 4

Suddenly, Lucia was yanked out of her own mind. She heard a voice that shook her to her core, with a timbre exactly like Felipe's. Lucia looked around for the source, and realized it was her great-grandson, who had returned to the Ranch. Maria was holding him in her arms, hurriedly striding towards Lucia in a plea for help. Lucia was happy to hear Horacio crying with a voice that didn't show the slightest hint of repression, fear, or shame. The child's vocal cords were absolutely free.

Horacio was bawling desperately, even though Maria had tried everything to make him stop. The baby had begun to cry on the drive back to the ranch. Chencha had been quick to suggest that the child's ears must be buzzing from all the bad thoughts he'd been subjected to. Maria had asked Chencha to please keep her opinions to herself, because she was anxious enough as it were. Like a stereotypical first-time mom, Maria didn't know what to do and was on the brink of a panic attack. Lucia took one glance at the boy, and she instantly knew he was suffering from an earache. She guided Maria into the kitchen, put a few drops of olive oil and a peeled garlic clove in a tablespoon, and placed it over an open flame until the garlic turned a golden brown. Then she sent Maria to fetch some cotton from her nightstand, and in the meantime, Lucia turned off the stove burner and stuck the spoon out the window. The change in temperature cooled the garlic and oil immediately. When Maria returned with the cotton, Lucia made a small ball of it and used it to absorb the oil so she could squeeze a few drops in her great-grandson's ear. She instructed Maria to hold the baby's head sideways to get better access to Horacio's ear.

"Grandma, do you know what you're doing?"

"I certainly do…this child has an earache."

"How do you know that? Wouldn't it be best to just take him to a doctor?"

"It would be best if you helped me. Can't you see your son is squirming from the pain and tilting his head to the side?"

It was at that moment that Maria noticed how Horacio had been trying to communicate his pain. She shut her mouth and did what her grandmother said, in awe of that matriarch who kept finding new ways to amaze Maria with her extensive knowledge. After a few minutes Horacio's pain subsided, and the child fell asleep. Maria left the boy in his crib and went to look for her grandmother, who despite the cold was out on the porch again, smoking another cigarette.

"Grandma..."

"Yes?"

"Do you have pictures of my mom with her dad?"

"I do."

"Can I see them?"

"Of course...but if you intend to send them to your sister, you're wasting your time. She won't believe you...She'll say the photograph has been altered."

"I know, she'll probably come up with something to dispute it. But I still want to send it, she has to believe me eventually..."

"People only see what they want to see. No matter how much proof you give her, she will resist. But come, I'll show you the pictures anyway."

Chapter 4

"As you are now, so once was I. As I am now, so you must be." This was a phrase that Lucia heard her mother repeat countless times. It's a popular saying that harbors a lot of wisdom, with a deeper meaning that refers to time, the eternal passerby that leaves its mark. And since Lucia believed that our lives involve more than the simple certainty that the passage of time will deteriorate our bodies, she decided not to repeat it. Especially because she doubted that Maria was capable of such a degree of introspection at the moment. Proof of this was her granddaughter's reaction when she saw Lucia and Felipe's wedding picture.

"Is this you, Grandma?" Maria had asked, not trying to hide her surprise even a little bit.

She hadn't recognized her. Lucia knew it was too much to ask of Maria, to imagine what her grandmother had looked like in her youth. At the most, she might understand that Lucia hadn't always looked the way she did now. But the Lucia that had lived in the past, unknown to Maria's eyes for so long, would never come to life in her granddaughter's mind even if she could see her in a photograph. We tend to think that only what we can see is real and alive, that everything that we didn't witness with our own two eyes—that didn't register in our memory—simply didn't exist. We can't recognize what we've never known. Nonetheless, the past lives on. It is a presence that interferes with our present lives in the most unexpected of ways. Like Horacio's birth.

The Lucia that was once was, still lived. Her present and past states may seem like two different people, but they're not. They're one and the same, vibrating with the equal intensity. And in order to see that Lucia, and recognize her, the spectator would need to look upon her with the knowledge of her background. Lucia regretted that everyone who had seen her grow, mature, and bloom was now dead, except for her friend Annie, whom she hadn't heard from in many, many years. Everyone else had died, and with them the memory of the Lucia that had once stirred desire in men, that had danced for nights on end, that had laughed, dreamed, and loved like few others did. She couldn't expect Maria to imagine that her grandmother had once been her age, that she once had long, shiny black hair. That her lips—now wrinkled from smoking so much—were once full of sensuality and could kiss an entire night away. That her now slow legs once moved in a steady stride and were frequently tangled in pleasure with someone else's thighs.

No, Maria's eyes saw other things, were interested in different matters. She admired the pictures of Lucia in her youth with surprise, but when she looked up, all she saw was an old woman who spent her time sitting on her back porch, smoking a cigarette with her eyes closed. Maria had no way of knowing that Lucia kept her eyes closed so she could see those who no longer have a body, but still live within her. They spoke to her, sang, and, whispered... Lucia saw them in her mind's eye as clearly as the first time. If Maria could even begin to imagine the intense carnal encounters her grandmother remembered during her quiet moments of contemplation, she would probably faint, and consider them obscene. If children aren't equipped to imagine their parents in acts of physical love, how can they ever consider their grandparents as sexual beings?

In a game of mirrors, Lucia observed Maria looking at the family pictures, and remembered herself in her granddaughter's body.

Not only that, she recognized in her the mannerisms, expressions and body language of some of her dead relatives. Both women saw completely different things in the photographs laid out on the carpet. Maria saw the proof that would restore her honor. Lucia saw the man she'd loved so much, the man with enormous, blazing eyes. The same eyes she saw in her great-grandson Horacio's. Felipe and Horacio's eyes were the same color, but had different sensibilities.

"No one ever looked at me like Felipe did. And no one has since," thought Lucia, and suddenly a horrible image crossed her mind: the last look in Felipe's eyes before he died.... before she killed him. Her mind went into panic mode, and she tried to evade the painful memory by thinking of the first time Felipe looked at her with love in his eyes. That look was so indelible that nothing or no one had ever been able to replace it. She remembered it clearly; it was the first time they'd seen each other, because Felipe had always lived in Chicago with his parents.

Felipe and his family had come back to Piedras Negras for Esperanza and Alex's wedding anniversary party. Esperanza and Alex were Lucia's parents. It had been a celebration full of emotion. Esperanza had refused to throw a party on that occasion for many years, because it also marked the day that her father, Pedro, and her aunt Tita had burned to death along with the original De La Garza Ranch. It was Esperanza's biggest loss, and it took her a long time to recover and accept that the death of Tita—the woman she considered to be her real mother—was also a reminder of the eternal love she'd shared with Pedro, outside of the restrictions of time and social norms. It was a day to celebrate the type of love that can melt two bodies together, the love that in one powerful blaze had forever bound Pedro and Tita's union with Alex and Esperanza's.

With that intention a party was planned, and many of the guests that were at Alex and Esperanza's wedding were invited. They had been spared from the fire due to the effects of Tita's banquet, which had ignited in them an irresistible urge to leave the party and make love. Of course, Gertrudis and her family made the trip from Chicago to enjoy the celebration, but no one could imagine that day would still surprise everyone.

As soon as Lucia and Felipe saw each other, they felt a strong connection. Felipe said hello and took her by the hand just as the band started to play his favorite song. Lucia laughed, and followed him to the dance floor. When Felipe gently put his arm around his cousin's waist, there was another powerful reaction. Lucia felt like she was floating, like she existed outside of space and time. They danced while the band sang *"Where or When"*.

Scan to listen to *Where or When*

Lucia didn't understand how or why, because she'd never met her cousin until that night, but her skin already knew the touch of Felipe's hands. It was as if she'd been caressed by them countless times before. Their bodies swayed to the rhythm of the music like they'd been rehearsing the choreography for months. Everything seemed familiar: Felipe's smile, the smell of his body, and especially the way he looked at her. His eyes. His large, blue eyes, in stark contrast to his chocolate skin. They made her forget the concept of time.

It was funny for Lucia to feel this sensation of familiarity with a man so different from anyone she'd known before. Felipe was dressed like he did in Chicago. The style of menswear in the years following World War II was characterized by high-waisted pants and jackets with wide lapels and large shoulder pads. Felipe's slim frame seemed to have been made for that style, making him even more attractive to Lucia. Felipe, on the other hand, felt intimidated being the center of attention. The only person in the room who made him feel at ease was Lucia, with whom he felt an immediately powerful and unexplainable connection.

Suddenly, during their dance, Lucia's locket fell from the silver chain that held it around her neck. It had been a fifteenth birthday present from her great-aunt Gertrudis. Before that, the locket had belonged to Mama Elena, Lucia's great-grandmother. Inside the locket were pictures of Mama Elena and a mulatto man who had been both the love of her life and Gertrudis' biological father. It was a magical moment when the locket, freed from its chain, fell to the ground. Both Lucia and Felipe kneeled down to pick it up at the same time. Their faces were just inches away, and they were powerless against the magnetic urge to share a kiss. A mighty electrical current shook Lucia from head to toe, and she felt an agonizing craving deep within her pelvis.

Maria's voice yanked Lucia back to the present:

"So, who was our first black ancestor?"

"José Treviño. His family came to Piedras Negras while fleeing from the American Civil War. Look, this is a picture of him…"

Lucia dug around the bottom of the trunk until she found an old notebook. She flipped through the pages until she found a picture of José Treviño to show Maria.

"How handsome…"

"Indeed, he was."

"And whose notebook was this?"

"This, child, was Tita's diary."

"And Tita was?"

"Your great-great-great aunt…"

"Hm," Maria said, feeling an unexplainable attraction to the old journal. "Can I borrow it?"

"Sure."

"Why is it all burned?"

"Well, it was the only thing that survived a fire that burned the entire ranch down…it's a long story, that will have to wait for another time. I'm feeling quite tired now."

Lucia wasn't really tired, she just wanted to close her eyes so she could travel back in time and enjoy Felipe once more. Maria put Tita's diary to the side and began to put the photographs back into her grandmother's trunk of memories. Before she closed it, she picked up a photograph that caught her eye. It was quite faded, and featured a gorgeous black woman standing in the middle of a cotton field. She had a kerchief on her head and was holding her apron with both hands, full of cotton flowers. Someone had written "Strange Fruit" on the back of the photograph.

"And who's this?"

"She was José Treviño's mother."

"Can I take this too?"

"Take everything you want…these photographs would've been lost to memory if not for your interest in them."

CHAPTER 5

Maria carefully observed Tita's face. Her ancestor's picture was in the first page of her diary. Maria couldn't believe that no one in her family had told her about Tita, and about the outrageous tradition that had kept her from taking a husband. As the youngest of three daughters, Tita had been destined to care for her mother until the latter's death. It was hard for Maria to understand this attitude of submissive obedience from her Twenty-First Century perspective. Although, if she was honest with herself, she had to admit that there were other forms of submission that still remained in place. People who belong to criminal groups or political parties have to obey their leaders, at the risk of being expelled, or worse. All sorts of organizations around the world follow a pyramidal structure. The ones at the top dictate orders, and the ones at the bottom carry them out. It's that simple—and terrifying. They obey without question, without dispute, without having an opinion and without realizing that the orders they so blindly follow are designed to turn them into victims of a system of oppression that decides what they can do, what they can eat, what type of education they have access to, even who they can love. Maria didn't see much of a difference between the oppressive mother figure that was Mama Elena and the oppressive system that rules the modern world. If a daughter gave up her right to marry in the past, in the present many still give up an opportunity to live a dignified life.

The Colors of My Past

What was wonderful about Tita's story was that she had found freedom in the kitchen. She had discovered a way to imprint loving energy in the food she prepared, and the formula to get away from the absurd rules that society and family tradition had imposed on her. She'd found an escape route and had even left behind a written guide. Tita's stirring testimony had made Maria cry, laugh, and think, but had also left thousands of questions in her mind. The historic document was fascinating. Maria read the entire diary in one sitting and despite having closed the notebook, she remained obsessed with Tita's expression. She couldn't get it out of her head. It was as if her ancestor was pleading for help in the photograph. Maria asked her grandmother if there were any other photos of Tita, and Lucia explained how there weren't many because of the fire that burned down the ranch and everything in it. The only thing that had survived the blaze was the diary, hidden under a metate. The only pictures of her that still existed had belonged to Tita's sister, Gertrudis. There weren't many. Tita could be found in some group photos taken during baptisms, family gatherings, and picnics, but that was it.

The picture in the diary showed Tita next to her mother, Maria's great-great-great-great-grandmother. That woman's gaze was icy cold and accusatory. After observing the photograph for a minute, María concluded that it reminded her of her own mother's, Luz Maria, who had apparently inherited Mama Elena's judging eyes. Few people could hold Luz Maria's reproachful gaze. Maria likened genes to a large chest we have inside us, but we're not aware of. Eye color, skin color, genetic diseases; all of these things could be found inside the chest, waiting to mix with another set of genes in order to surprise us and make us wonder "where did those blue eyes come from? Or that curly hair, that dark skin?" What absurd necessity compels these wayward genes to wander aimlessly for generations just to pop up suddenly and disrupt our lives? Who dictated their orders? What laws govern them? What has the power to activate information that can remain dormant for so long? Maria was terrified to think of all the unknown information that coursed through her veins. She had a hard time coming to terms with the idea of being a walking receptacle for genetic information from the most distant of ancestors, information that included all kinds of fears, prejudice, and guilt. Maria carried this within her the way one keeps the memory of a night of passion, the smell of roses, or the taste of chocolate.

Reading the diary awakened in Maria an incontrollable urge to eat. She made her way to the kitchen, even though it was four in the morning. Horacio was sleeping placidly in his crib, so she decided it would be okay to leave him alone for just a moment. She was starving. Maria was beginning to accept that she might have an eating disorder, but she didn't know what to do about it. Back when she lived in Mexico City—which seemed a lifetime ago—she'd tried to go on a diet. Every morning Maria would begin a juice fast. At first, her body seemed to adjust well to it. She felt energized, and not hungry at all during the day. But as soon as she went to bed, her troubles began. She had nightmares of secret desires and food. Maria would then sleepwalk and make her way to the kitchen and open the fridge. Only then would she realize she was out of bed, but it was already too late. She'd already devoured everything in sight. This habit became even worse at Lucia's house, because her grandmother's kitchen was host to all sorts of delicacies and temptations.

Maria trusted herself less each day. Consciously, she wished with all her soul to recover her figure and lose the extra weight she'd gained during the pregnancy, but as soon as she fell asleep her subconscious took over and made her do all the things she didn't want to do. The following morning, she would wake up with an awful emotional hangover, and would swear that today she'd stick to the diet. Instead of eating what she really craved for breakfast, like huevos rancheros with chilaquiles, she would make a juice. The recipe was spinach, red berries, an apple, and some nuts. After drinking the juice, she felt great and was confident that she'd make it to the next day without binge eating. Maria actually liked the diet, because it made her eat things she normally wouldn't. She never ate apples, for example. She considered the fruit a waste of time, with all the chewing. But if she juiced the apple, she could get all of its nutrients in a few big gulps. Maria would spend all day juice fasting and feeling healthier by the minute. Before she went to bed, she'd pat herself on the back, proud of having controlled her appetite. She would get under the covers with a clear conscience, her self-esteem through the roof. But as soon as she closed her eyes, images of cakes, tacos, sandwiches, and tamales began to parade through her mind. Unable to resist, Maria would inevitably break her own promise to herself, and felt like the biggest failure. It was at that exact moment, as she was crossing the threshold of defeat at five in the morning, that the kitchen door opened, and a very fresh Lucia walked in. Her days always began that early. Lucia saw everything her granddaughter had eaten, the proof lay scattered across the table; chocolate wrappers, crumbs…She turned to Maria and bluntly asked her:

"Didn't anyone teach you how to knit?"

"No…"

"What about embroidery?"

"Of course not."

Maria took one last bite of the pastry she was holding, and as she wiped her mouth with her sleeve, she thought about the absurd question her grandmother had just asked. She didn't understand what her point was, especially so early in the morning.

Maria and her grandmother sat together, knitting with enthusiasm. They had begun before dawn and showed no signs of slowing down even though it was almost time for the midday meal. Time was flying by.

Knitting turned out to be quite a revelation for Maria. She never learned to knit because she had thought it more important to develop her intellect and get a graduate degree. Maria had always believed that knitting was something old women did because they had nothing else to do. Although in retrospect, she had to admit that all the academic knowledge she'd acquired had never brought her peace. Maybe there was a different type of knowledge, an ancestral wisdom that Maria had yet to find, probably because she had always searched in the wrong places. This wisdom wouldn't be found in books. It was hidden in plain sight, at the core of intimate, everyday activities that had been cast aside by academics. She was now beginning to understand why knitting had given humans a purpose for thousands of years. We knit with the intention to clothe, to create rope, to tell stories and represent symbols in textiles. A long time ago men would knit as well, as did children. Knitting is a manifestation of the creation myth.

With great joy, Maria discovered that as long as she made the needles dance in in her hands, she didn't think about food at all. Or about what she would say to her bitch of a sister next time she saw her, or about the look of contempt she planned to give Carlos when they signed the divorce papers. When Maria had received a message from Carlos' lawyer the previous night asking for a divorce, she had been so outraged that she didn't even cry. As her grandmother had wisely said; that man didn't deserve a single tear, nor a single thought from her. That was part of why she found knitting so absorbing. She didn't have to concentrate on anything but the knit and the purl. As if through magic, the world disappeared and little by little a garment would take form, designed to clothe her son, no less. To bundle him up with warmth, to show him that her love for him was so big that it could more than make up for the lack of affection from the rest of the family. Knitting for her son was…

"Grandma, did you knit for my mom?"

"Of course. Before she was even born, I was knitting for her. I always made her something special on her birthday and for Christmas…until she stopped talking to me, of course."

Maria thought about that last Christmas at Lucia's house, and faintly remembered the sweater her mom had received as a gift. Luz Maria never wore it, but before she died, she asked Maria to fetch her the sweater, because she wanted to wear it when she was discharged from the hospital. She died before Maria even got a chance to bring it to her.

"Did you teach her how to knit?"

"Who?"

"My mom."

"I did. And she was very good at it."

Without meaning to, Maria put herself in the role of her own therapist and began an inner dialogue:

"Why do you think your mother never taught you how to knit?" Maria the therapist asked.

And Maria the patient answered herself:

"Because she didn't want to think about her mother. She decided to get as far away as she could, from her and from everything she represented."

"Do you think she avoided passing on that knowledge to you so she wouldn't see her own mother reflected in you?"

"That's probably right."

"And what about you? Why didn't you show any interest in learning how to knit? Why were you so obsessed with school?"

"Obviously because I wanted to be like my mom...I wanted her to be proud of me, proud of my intellect..."

And then she blurted out loud:

"Wow! I'll even save money on therapy..."

Lucia looked up at her granddaughter but made no comment and just continued to knit. Maria didn't take her grandmother's silence personally, because she was just beginning to realize how much of an absorbing activity knitting was. All morning she'd done nothing but knit, except for the short break she took to feed Horacio. Knitting relaxed her completely. She was beginning to recognize it as a form of meditation, of finding peace. There was no doubt that her grandmother was wise. At this difficult moment in Maria's life, when everyone had cast her aside with disdain, knitting had emerged as a way for her to get her bearings, to stay afloat, to put her thoughts in order, and to control her anxiety. She discovered that while knitting, one could hold wonderful conversations with oneself, with others, or just share a comfortable silence. The activity was so enthralling that Maria didn't even think to check her Facebook feed, read her emails, or get into dumb and brutally aggressive fights on twitter.

Maria was grateful that her grandmother was teaching her to knit. She was sure that it would become a milestone in her life. Until that day, Maria and her grandmother were just two strangers that shared blood, but now they were knitting bonds of affection and cementing a marvelous complicity between them, without the need to speak. When evening rolled along, Lucia asked Maria if she would like to listen to some music. Maria nodded, and Lucia played a vinyl record she fetched from a trunk. The music of Billie Holiday filled Lucia's study, which everyone still referred to by the name Mama Elena had given it: the dark room. The name was now vestigial, because the room was filled with light during most of the day. This was because it was no longer the original room. It was a reconstruction of what had been Mama Elena's bath. After Mama Elena died, Tita moved in and used the room as a lab, study, kitchen, bath, and even bedroom. Tita had left the bathtub in the middle of the room because she liked the idea of taking baths right there, in the same spot where she and Pedro had made love for the first time. Throughout the years the room had been rebuilt and remodeled several times. The first time it had been rebuilt was after the great fire that burned down the ranch in the 1930s. Esperanza, Maria's great grandmother, wanted the ranch to be rebuilt as an exact replica, especially the dark room. Along one of the walls there was a kitchenette and a sink with a drain board where wrought-iron pans coexisted with test-tubes and microscopes. Lucia's only addition to the room was an altar where she kept a photograph of Felipe. Every day she would place a fresh bouquet of red carnations in a black vase on the altar. The room was a magic place, definitely one-of-a-kind. It was a place for encounters, transformations, and contact with the light. Lucia didn't remember exactly when she'd decided to use oil lamps to light and heat the room. The lamps provided both warmth, and a soft light that was especially conducive for knitting.

Lucia and Maria, grandmother and granddaughter, sat knitting and listening to music in what had been Mama Elena's dark room, the place where that powerful woman bathed in the darkness, the place where Tita lost her virginity, and later on—during a hot chocolate bath—finally reconciled with her mother. It was the same room where Lucia and Felipe gave in to their lust for each other, where Felipe died, where Tita and Pedro had loved one another so intensely that they caught on fire and returned to the light.

Scan to listen to *I'll Be Seeing You*

Lucia and Maria listened to Billie Holiday sing "I'll Be Seeing You" as they weaved a memorable story together. The room was a place that had a vocation to strip souls bare, to light them on fire, to host rituals where darkness gives way to light, where song has the power to bring forth long-repressed emotions and transmute them into tears that cleanse the soul. Bringing hidden things out into the light will forever be an act of liberation and healing. Grandmother and granddaughter healed, letting their tears fall onto their knitting. Lucia, still without saying a word, gave Maria a tissue and continued crying. Maria didn't ask her grandmother why she wept.

It was obvious that, just like Maria, Lucia cried for a man who was no longer with her, at least in physical form. Maria needed only to observe how her grandmother honored the memory of Grandpa Felipe to understand this. The ritual that began with changing the red carnations in the vase every morning, the devotion with which she dusted the piano that had belonged to Esperanza and that had been played by Felipe... Maria's grandfather was present in the sheet music, in his ties, hats, and handkerchiefs, in every object that once belonged to him and that Lucia kept and treasured. Lucia had a trunk full of affections and a mind plagued with images that were reanimated by music. Through sound and light is how one recovers what is loved. But the two women had forgotten about the real, physical presence that was in the room with them among all the other invisible ones, until it manifested itself with a loud cry as Horacio filled every last inch of the dark room with his powerful voice, drowning out the music. He demanded to be fed. The child's cry was an announcement, an omen, an affirmation that within him dwelled all the men that were loved and had been loved by the women in his family. In his genes, Pedro, John, Juan, Alex, Felipe, and Carlos lived on.

Knitting quickly became a daily activity for Maria. She would sit with her grandmother in the afternoons, and they would knit and listen to music. On one occasion, before Lucia played one of her vinyl records, Maria surprised her by playing a song she had downloaded on her tablet. It was from a record by Jimmy Yancey, the great blues pianist that Felipe had met and had even become friends with. That version of the song had originally appeared on one of Felipe's favorite records. During one of their passionate fights, Lucia had thrown the black disc at Felipe's head, but the man ducked, and the vinyl had smashed to pieces against the wall. They were never able to find another copy. Lucia's eyes welled with tears as the song began to play.

"Where did you find this?" she asked her granddaughter.

"Online."

"But that record is impossible to find, I've been searching for years. I…broke mine."

"Yeah Grandma, but nowadays you can find almost everything on iTunes. it doesn't exactly sound like a vinyl record, but at least you have access to all the music in the world…"

"And how do I get access to it?"

"You have to buy a computer, or a tablet, or at least a smartphone. Then you have to get an internet connection in the ranch, and I can show you how."

Chapter 5

"Well, what are we waiting for? Let's get the internet hooked up!"

"But Grandma, we were just about to start our knitting session…"

"Who are you and what have you done with my granddaughter?" Lucia joked. "Weren't you the one who was dying to get internet here?"

Maria laughed. "Alright. Let's do it. "

Lucia authorized the installation of high-speed internet on her property, and as soon as the connection was completed, the onrush of data radically changed life at the ranch.

Exceeding all expectations, even her own, Lucia learned how to handle the novel technology in one afternoon. With her perfect grasp on the world of the invisible, sending and receiving information was nothing new to her.

The arrival of the internet at the ranch was quite an occurrence. Maria was now able to instantly message people whenever she wanted, and when the occasion called for it—which was often—send insults to her sister. Chencha discovered that she could see photographs of her grandchildren on Facebook, so she began to spend all her free time sharing videos and commenting on everyone's posts. Everyone was suddenly involved in everyone else's affairs.

One day, a woman called Betty Miller messaged Lucia on Facebook. Betty was the great granddaughter of one of Lucia's relatives. The purpose of her message was to invite Lucia to a party that was being organized for Annie Thompson's eighty-fifth birthday. Annie's maiden name was Brown, and that was how Lucia remembered her. Annie had not only been Lucia's best friend growing up, but she was also her aunt. She was the daughter of John and Shirley, Lucia's grandparents. Annie was four years older than Lucia, but nobody could tell the difference. They grew up sharing everything; toys, food, friends, and records. Lucia was very excited to receive the invitation, and immediately RSVPd. She hadn't heard from Annie in a long time, and now, thanks to the internet, they would be reunited.

Walking into the ballroom on the day of the party was like walking through a time portal. The theme was the 1940s, and all the decorations reflected that era. Every guest—no matter their age—was also dressed accordingly. The objective of the party was to make Annie feel like she'd returned to her heyday, and the planners certainly accomplished their goal. There was a live band playing classics by Tommy Dorsey, Benny Goodman, Glenn Miller, and Count Basie. Lucia felt like it was her party too. At first Lucia had been very excited to be invited, and had been looking forward to the party, but as the days went by, she began to dread the thought of facing her family and old friends and having to address her daughter's death. How would she ever explain the fact that no one had notified her? How would she hide the fact that they hadn't spoken in years?

Despite this, Maria had talked her grandmother into going, with a simple argument:

"Grandma, do you think your old friends whom you haven't seen in ages knew that you and mom weren't on speaking terms? Come on! They probably don't even know mom passed away. You should really, go. In fact, I'll take you! We'll have so much fun… after the horrible shit we went through a couple of weeks ago, we totally deserve to party."

Chapter 5

Maria was right, both women needed a distraction. From the moment she'd dug out a couple of dresses from her trunk of memories—one for her, and one for Maria—Lucia had embarked on a joyous journey into her past. And when they stepped into the ballroom, all of her fears and physical ailments disappeared.

Lucia felt like the protagonist in the movie "Orchestra Wives," which she'd seen at least 20 times with Annie. Despite the passing of time, both women still maintained a marvelous appearance. They both looked stunning that night. As soon as they saw each other, they embraced with great joy. Annie was full of laughter and was enjoying her wonderful surprise party. The wind from the band's brass section swept up both women like a hurricane that washed away the years. Lucia and Annie let their feet lead them to the center of the dance floor, where they spent the better part of the night dancing like the years had never passed.

And in the middle of the roaring music and crowds dancing, Maria heard a laughter that shook her to the core, and once again made her feel like she was in a Broadway show. The singer of the band was belting out "Some Enchanted Evening", but despite the amplification it wasn't enough to drown the laughter that caught Maria's attention. It sounded so familiar! She knew she'd heard it before but couldn't remember where exactly.

Scan to listen to *Some Enchanted Evening*

Suddenly, Maria remembered who that distinctive laugh belonged to. It was Dr. Miller! He was with a group of people who had approached Annie Thompson to congratulate her. Maria walked in their direction, and Dr. Miller saw her. He walked towards her as well, and time stopped for the two of them.

"Dr. Miller?" Maria asked.

"Maria? What are you doing here?" said the doctor, in genuine surprise.

"I'm here with my grandma," answered Maria, pointing to Lucia.

"Don't tell me you're Lucia's granddaughter! That means your mother was her daughter…did you know we're distant cousins?"

"I didn't, but I'd rather not hear about it right now, Doctor. I'd much rather dance."

Dr. Miller laughed heartily once more and didn't hesitate. He took Maria by the hand and led her to the dance floor.

Lucia watched her granddaughter dance with Dr. Roberto Miller, while the band played "As Time Goes By." They made a perfect couple. They'd been dancing for a while now and had forgone all formalities between them. Just by observing how Roberto had taken Maria by the waist and pulled her in, and how Maria had softly let her body come into contact with his, Lucia knew the inevitable outcome. She would know, since she'd made love to Felipe the first time they met! Her eyes swelled with tears from the tender love she was witnessing, a love that touched her heart.

Lucia thought about how ridiculous it is to think that love can end, that it has an expiration date, that it can die…One just needs to see a couple that looks into each other's eyes like Roberto and

Maria, to understand the flaw in that way of thinking. Love is eternal; it can travel and transform, but it always returns. It is reincarnated every day into new bodies, new mouths, new hands, and we should be grateful for every one of its manifestations. Lucia thought that we should all be a conduit for love, greet it with open hearts, and bless it. And so, fulfilling the role of "Guardian of the Fire" that her grandfather John had bestowed upon her when she was but a child, Lucia walked to the dance floor and approached Roberto and Maria while the band played "Stardust." She told them to enjoy the party for as long as they wanted, because she was heading back to the ranch and she'd be happy to look after Horacio. Maria thanked her grandmother enthusiastically, and Roberto promised he'd drive Maria home himself.

Lucia's generous offer opened the doors to freedom. Maria and Roberto closed the space between them once more, and their bodies shot off sparks of pure desire. Maria felt the Doctor's member grow hard against her thigh. She never thought that her body could elicit such a response from a man like Doctor Miller. Maria felt fat and unattractive, but that didn't stop her from wanting to behave very, very badly. For many years she had wondered what it even meant to be "well behaved". At her parent's house, it meant obeying, doing whatever she was told. Behaving badly meant acting in any way that was unexpected, making her own decisions, especially if they were considered politically or socially incorrect. Maria understood Lucia's offer as permission to misbehave, and she wasn't going to let her grandmother down.

Lucia turned on her heel and walked away from the dancing couple with a huge grin on her face. She knew that one thing would lead to another, that they would go from dancing to embracing, from embracing to kissing, from kissing to fondling, and from fondling to penetration. What she couldn't imagine was how long it would take Maria and Roberto to climax, because when they arrived at Roberto's hotel room, they took their sweet time just making out and touching one another. They exchanged long and deep kisses, as if Roberto Miller could sense Maria's hesitation to expose her chubby body and large midsection. With patience and barely contained passion, Roberto gave her all the time she needed to strip herself of all her fears and insecurities. Maria hadn't made love in a long time. A month before Horacio was born, she and Carlos had suspended all sexual activities, and they had not been intimate at all after the birth. They'd hardly spoken to each other for their last month together, before he abandoned her. Since then Maria had been observing an involuntary vow of celibacy, which she was determined to break spectacularly.

Roberto's mouth moved from Maria's lips to her breasts. He kissed and kneaded them, then sucked on her nipples like no one had ever done before. This made Maria drift away for an instant, remembering that she'd read in Tita's diary how her great-great-great-aunt had been able to breastfeed her nephew without ever having been pregnant. After reading that, Maria had searched on the internet and had found that indeed, with the right stimulation, a woman who has never been pregnant can produce milk. She had been trying unsuccessfully to breastfeed her child for so long, but that night, thanks to Doctor Miller's mouth, her breasts began to swell and leak milk. She considered this a miracle of love. Her breasts—like Tita's many years before—bloomed in the lips of a man who shared the same name as her ancestor's nephew: Roberto, the son of Rosaura and Pedro, whom Tita had so lovingly fed. Maria looked forward to returning to the ranch and surprising her son with the good news.

But that wasn't the only surprise Maria would encounter. The next morning, when Roberto drove her back to the ranch, they found Chencha waiting in the driveway. She signaled for them to pull over, and Maria felt a pang of fear deep in her stomach.

"What is it, Chencha?" she asked, alarmed.

"Nothing, it's just that your grandma asked me to come warn you that Mister Carlos is in the house, waiting to speak to you. Your grandma had to tell him you were in the shower. She is entertaining him in the kitchen, and thinks it best for you to come in through the back door so he doesn't notice…"

"Carlos? Is that Horacio's dad?" asked Roberto.

"Yeah. I'd better just jump out here."

Roberto nodded, but before Maria got out of his car, he took her by the hand and said:

"I know you have a decision to make. Whatever it is, I will respect it. If this helps in any way, I want you to know that I've never wanted to spend the rest of my life with anyone, until last night. It may sound very sudden and unexpected, but it is what it is. That's all."

"Okay" Maria said, and got out of the car with tears in her eyes.

Chapter 6

Maria rushed up the stairs, flung off her dress, and ran to Horacio. Her breasts were about to burst, but the stars were not in her favor, because the child was out cold and she couldn't feed him. She had no choice but to face Carlos with swollen breasts. Maria could've benefitted from some time to calm her emotions, but she decided she'd rather just get it over with.

When Maria walked into the kitchen, she found Carlos in the middle of a placid conversation with her grandmother. Husband and wife greeted each other coldly. Maria was gorgeous, she glowed with sexual satisfaction and self-realization. Her eyes shone brighter than ever, and her hair was loose, settled in its natural curls.

"Did you do something to your hair?" Carlos asked. "You look great."

"No, I just didn't straighten it today," Maria answered matter-of-factly.

"I didn't know it was so curly…"

"There's a lot of things you don't know about me."

Lucia took that answer as her cue to leave the kitchen. She knew they needed to be alone so they could speak freely. She excused herself, and asked Carlos to help her up from her seat, because her sciatica was acting up. She had been leaning down to put Horacio back in his crib after feeding him his bottle, when Chencha burst in the room in a panic to inform Lucia of the situation. Her entire body tensed up. The last she'd heard from Maria had been at about five A.M. Her granddaughter had called to apologize for having fallen asleep at Roberto's, and then to ask if she could give Horacio his bottle, because they wouldn't make it back to the ranch in time. Maria promised to shower quickly and be back as soon as she could, which turned out to be more than two hours later! This was because Maria and Roberto got in the shower together, where he tenderly lathered her up with soap, kissed her from head to toe after rinsing her off, and they inevitably made love once more. Lucia didn't judge them! She even sympathized, a veteran in the arts of arousal and intimacy between couples herself, but they'd certainly put her in a tough spot with their delay. With great pain, she made her way down the stairs to entertain Carlos until her granddaughter arrived. Lucia didn't want this Carlos—whom she hadn't had the pleasure to meet until that day—to know that Maria had spent the night somewhere else and use it as an excuse to label her granddaughter a whore.

Lucia would have wanted to walk faster, but the pain in her hips held her back. Maria and Carlos remained silent during the time it took the older woman to leave the room.

As soon as Lucia was out of earshot, Carlos broke the silence:

"Maria, please forgive me…I had no idea about your…"

"No, Carlos," she interrupted, "this isn't about being misinformed. Horacio's birth wasn't some leak you read about on the internet. This is a human being we're talking about! Your own son! And you, and me…"

"I know Maria, but try to understand. It was hard for me to come to terms with…" He tried to talk over her, but Maria raised her voice:

Chapter 6

"With having a black son? Or with the realization that I was always faithful, that I once loved you with all my heart? What was it so hard to come to terms with?" Maria was now yelling at the top of her lungs. Tears of rage rolled down her cheeks. She furiously wiped them off and turned around so Carlos wouldn't see her cry. He approached her from behind and tried to hug her, as he asked:

"Why did you say you once loved me? Don't you love me anymore?"

Maria pushed him away violently. Horacio, awakened by his mother yelling, began to cry.

"Can I see him, Maria?" asked Carlos.

"Why? To see if he looks like you?" she replied sardonically.

"Come on Maria, please don't be like that. I'm here because I want to fix our relationship. I don't want to lose you."

"Well, you're too late. You've lost me. Did you bring the divorce papers?"

"No…"

"Well, just mail them to me so I can sign them and be done with this. Now, please leave."

"I'm not going anywhere until I see my son," Carlos began, just as Chencha interrupted with the baby in her arms.

"Good morning, I'm sorry to interrupt but the child is hungry. Should I give him his bottle?"

"No, thank you, Chencha. I'll take him," Maria said. She picked up the child, but before she could leave the room, Carlos stopped her.

"Please Maria, don't make me beg. Let me hold my son."

Maria couldn't deny him this. She knew it was Carlos' right to hold Horacio, and she also wanted to give her child the opportunity to be held by his biological father. The moment was awkward. Carlos didn't have the slightest clue how to hold a baby. The child felt uncomfortable, and cried harder. It wasn't at all like what she'd always imagined, but Maria was still moved to see Carlos weep as he held Horacio. Nevertheless, it was too little, too late. That past night, Maria had lived something that she could never forget. Minutes ago, she was certain that she wanted to spend the rest of her life with Roberto. She could still taste him , still felt him deep within her. But seeing her penitent husband ask for forgiveness, seeing him vulnerable and with his guard down, really confused her.

Maria took Horacio back and asked Carlos to wait in the living room while she fed the boy. Horacio couldn't have been happier to be finally drinking his mother's milk straight from the source. He drank so fast, he almost choked. Maria couldn't tell what brought her more relief: being able to breastfeed her child, or letting the contained milk out of her swollen breast. Whatever the reason, she owed it to Roberto. She thought of him, and felt her stomach shrink. Maria had a big decision to make, and the uncertainty filled her with fear. What if she made the wrong choice? She came to no conclusion that day. After talking to Carlos at length, she asked him to give her time to clear her mind. She argued that she was not in the correct mental state to make any decisions, which was true. Carlos left the ranch under the agreement that he could return in a month's time. As soon as he left, Maria immediately went back to her room and rushed to open Tita's diary at the part where she cancels her wedding hours before it was to take place. She took a pencil and underlined the passage that read: "I turned and rushed into the house so I didn't have to watch him leave. There will never be anyone like John." The first time she read the diary, Maria had thought she'd never want to be in Tita's shoes when she had to make that decision. Now she found herself in a similar dilemma. She was sure that Roberto—who was incidentally John's great-grandson—was an extraordinary man. She didn't want to let him go, and didn't want history to repeat itself. On the other hand there was Carlos, her husband, the man whose child she bore. Their marriage had been idyllic up until Horacio's birth. She had one month to choose one over the other.

It was three in the morning, and the moon was full. Maria sat at the window, watching the clear sky with a mug of hot chocolate Lucia had made her before going to bed. Her grandmother knew Maria would stay up all night. The entire night sky was visible from Maria's bedroom window. This was a privilege that she never enjoyed in her apartment back in Mexico City, despite it being a "luxury" unit. Maria was enthralled by the moon. It was the same moon that Tita looked upon the night when her sister Gertrudis ran away from the ranch on horseback. It was the same moon under which José Treviño wrote his goodbye letter to Mama Elena, the love of his life. The same moon that bore witness to weddings and separations, to laughter, to weeping, the same moon that makes the oceans rise and guides women's menstrual cycles. Maria thought about how absurd life can become in big cities, where one loses track of the moon's phases, not to mention where in the sky it rises and where it sets. Having the opportunity to observe the movement of the stars while drinking chocolate stirred something deep within Maria. Her entire body was vibrating, from the tip of her toes to her top of her head. And complimentary to the vibration, she felt her head pounding to the rhythm of the stars. Maria could feel the stars penetrate her skin, like she'd opened a channel of communication that allowed her to feel, listen to, and understand the Cosmos as it softly whispered in her ear. The silence of the early morning hours was such that Maria could hear her chocolate-powered heart beating loudly, but most surprisingly, she began to hear the heartbeat of the Universe itself. She wondered if her grandmother hadn't slipped some substance in the drink, because she could clearly feel—as if tripping on hallucinogens—that her pulse and that of the Cosmos became one, breathing and thinking in unison. Thousands of answers appeared in her mind before she even had the time to ask questions. Maria was holding a digital conversation with the heavens. She had learned from Lucia that everything that moves—from a star to a microscopic life form—emits a vibration and a sound. The planet Earth itself emits its own distinctive and unique voice that harmonizes with that of the other celestial spheres. If we were able to listen to this voice, to perceive it, we would understand that its sound connects us to her, and to the rest of the universe, at all times. Its pulse will always be an invitation to be deciphered and understood. But how? By attuning. To be in tune is to vibrate with the same frequency as another tone. Upon reaching this conclusion, Maria was assailed by a deep concern: if Horacio had been listening to her heartbeat for the nine months he spent in her womb, he must be in tune with her, because they'd formed part of the same universe of shared emotions, genetic information and knowledge. That would mean that now, the child was probably suffering from the same sadness and confusion as she was, right?

It was then that Maria thought she heard her grandfather's voice inside her head, and she had a powerful vision of a group of slaves taken from Africa, traveling deep inside the bowels of a slave ship, unable to look up at the night sky. They had been denied the moon, the sun, their mothers, their home, and had lost their voice, which inevitably faded from their throats as a result of such heartrending separation. She thought of the first nights when those prisoners observed the moon from other lands, and deduced that maybe the road to finding what had been lost could be to recover that voice, that powerful and painful voice whose singing has the power stir us to our very core.

All of this was happening at the speed of light. Maria became aware that no matter what she focused on, she could still see and hear everything. She felt a part of everything and everyone. Maria tried to look inwards and concentrate on herself, to find an answer to the question she'd asked a few seconds before: how had her own voice changed since her son's birth? The answer came to her mind in less than a heartbeat: just as birds change their song depending on the season, a woman "sounds" different depending on the time of day, or on the emotion that that drives her. If we consider emotions to be an energy that can modify everything around it, then Maria's voice had obviously undergone a significant change, especially in the past twenty-four hours. While in Roberto's presence she was a lively symphony, but then deteriorated into a sad and lonely accordion the moment she saw Carlos.

Every time Maria had a thought, she instantly connected with the subject or object of her thought. It was as if her mind were typing the thoughts into the fastest search engine in existence. If everything is interconnected, does that mean that when one person cries, the entire Universe cries as well? And what if someone laughs? Maria missed the answer to that query, because Horacio had woken up, loud and joyful. His babbling was like a beautiful song. Maria approached her baby and mimicked an improvised gibberish song back to him. For a few minutes, mother and son communicated musically. In that moment Maria felt music was a way to absorb the entire Universe, and she remembered a song that her father used to sing to her when she was a child: "When You're Smiling." He had heard it in Frank Sinatra's rendition. She finally understood that musical laughter, like that of our hearts, is able to make everyone in its vicinity smile. It's such a powerful neurotransmitter that it can be considered the true food of love, carrying information from one place to the other, from one time to another, from person to person, from universe to universe, from room to room. Lucia, in her own bedroom, began to harmonize with Maria, like a guitar string that vibrates when the same note is strummed on a different guitar that is nearby, and she also smiled. Grandmother, granddaughter and great-grandson, three beings in tune, smiled along with all the stars in the universe.

Scan to listen to *When You're Smiling*

That sweet smile rescued Lucia from her recurring nightmares. She always had the same two, horrible dreams. The first one was a replay of the night that Felipe became paralyzed. In her dream they were leaving the nightclub where Felipe sang on the weekends. As they walked toward their parked car, Felipe was tense, angry even, resentful that Lucia had pressured him into taking that job. He hated singing in front of crowds. They were arguing, so they didn't notice a drunk man approaching them. When he was only a few feet away, the drunk man asked:

"Excuse me, can I have your autograph?"

Felipe, exasperated, said yes, to which the man replied:

"I wasn't asking you. I was asking her. It must be a feat to be married to such a shitty singer."

Felipe snapped, and punched the man. As they walked away, the assailant pulled out a gun and shot Felipe in the back.

The sound of the gunshot ended the nightmare, and the second one began, the one where she dreamed she was deaf. In that nightmare, Lucia remembered clearly the moment of Felipe's last breath. And after his death rattle, Lucia was invaded by an absolute, monumentally painful silence. That was her memory of the morning her husband died, the deafening sensation of having lost Felipe's voice forever. The nightmare concluded with her running down an open field, covering her ears with both hands, like the figure in Munch's "The Scream."

Lucia felt grateful to have been pulled out of that painting, out of that deadly dream. Waking up from a nightmare brings tremendous relief. If only we could cast aside our fears, guilt, and remorse with such ease. If only all horrors could disappear from our lives by the simple act of opening our eyes, waking up to the certainty of never having hurt anyone, never having denied anyone forgiveness, never having killed anyone. If only every horror in our lives could be nothing but a bad dream that we could easily wake up from.

Lucia held the belief that one of the major deterrents to healing a broken relationship was lack of forgiveness. To deny the act of forgiveness is to give up on magic, alchemy, and transformation. We choose to see the other as nothing but the guilty party that deserves our eternal punishment, instead of the forgiveness which would grant them a fresh start. Lucia often wondered how it was possible that her own daughter never forgave her, when she'd been raised in a home where the act of forgiveness was a constant practice that tore down the walls that anger and incomprehension might build.

To deny forgiveness was to give up on the possibility that the other could become something different than what we expected, it was to deny life itself, because life is never just a single, permanent, static moment. Everything is in constant flux. Anything can change in the blink of an eye. That was one of Lucia's passions, to be a witness of change, to see the look of wonder in other's faces as they discovered something they'd never seen before. That was why she pressured Felipe so much into singing in public. When Felipe sang he transcended his status as a man of mixed race to become an exceptional singer that awakened desire in women and admiration in men. When Felipe sang, Lucia felt important. She became Lucia, the wife of Felipe, the man with the prodigious voice. The change in how Felipe was perceived changed her as well, filling her with satisfaction. The same thing happened when

Luz Maria grew up and became a professional; Lucia became the mother of Luz Maria, the famous biologist.

It hurt Lucia to think of her daughter. She was truly sorry she hadn't seen Luz Maria before her death. Even though they never patched things up between them in real life, in Lucia's dreams they were closer than ever. In the dreamscape, Lucia could hug and kiss Luz Maria, and feel tremendously comforted. Lucia had the ability to control her dreams and turn them into something more real than life itself. She first discovered this ability after the accident that made Felipe a paraplegic. In respect to their sex life, at first it was enough for them to disrobe, kiss, and touch each other to be sexually satisfied. They both knew that that making love was not only about bodies. But after several years, all the resources they turned to—tongues, fingers, erotic fantasies— came up short. Something was missing for Lucia. That was when she began to dream of the other Felipe, the one who existed before the accident. Before long she discovered that in her dreams she could reach the most phenomenal orgasms with him. She could decide upon a place, setting, and costumes—or lack thereof—in which their sexual encounters would take place, and Felipe played his role to perfection, satisfying her completely. It was with her eyes closed that Lucia could recover Felipe and see him, smell him, taste him, and enjoy him madly.

Lucia never thought that her ability to dream lucidly would eventually bring about so much trouble in her life. Her only motivation came from the need to find a solution to the physical limitation imposed by Felipe's paralysis. Since she was a child, Lucia suspected there must be a way to escape the material condition. As she grew, she came to experience this escape herself. She had her grandfather John to thank for the realization that we can leave our bodies by way of our imagination. Thoughts travel outside the body, and they can take us with them. Her grandfather was a veritable well of knowledge. Esperanza, Lucia's mother, had been a concert pianist so successful that she frequently toured the world, and her father Alex was a well-respected lawyer who could afford to travel with his wife, so Lucia spent a lot of time with her paternal grandparents John and Shirley. Lucia had the fondest memories of this time, and of all the knowledge her elders instilled in her. She particularly remembered one Sunday morning when her grandparents took her to church. Shirley helped her get dressed, putting a nylon petticoat on the young Lucia, under a beautiful white dress with pink bows that had been purchased for the occasion. Lucia bounced along the road, filled with self-satisfaction, but after a few yards the petticoat began to ride up her legs. Lucia told her grandfather she wanted to go back home, because she was very uncomfortable. John took his granddaughter by the hand and headed back to the house. He asked Shirley to help Lucia take off the petticoat and asked to have it brought to the kitchen. He carried Lucia and sat her on the edge of the kitchen sink, then instructed her to hold the petticoat up high in her left hand, and to hold on to the water faucet with her right. John opened the faucet, and the water began to flow. He asked the young Lucia to picture the electric energy from the petticoat flowing through her body, leaving through her right hand and then going down the drain with the water. To Lucia's surprise, the petticoat—which moments before was crackling and shocking her—showed no more signs of static electricity. The electrical charge was gone, carried away by the water. Later, John explained to her that water is the best conductor. Lucia was marveled to learn that there's energy that can affect matter, but not permanently. It comes and goes, can pierce bodies, and travel far.

"Grandpa, but the water didn't take any of my energy, did it?"

"No, it only took the electromagnetic energy that your body generated as your legs rubbed against the nylon."

That day Lucia not only learned that energy coursed through her at all times, but most importantly, that energy can be channeled and controlled at will. Well, she never came to dominate that last part. Even as an adult, Lucia always had trouble with the electricity her body generated. She wasn't able to control it and was never able to wear any kind of petticoat or pantyhose. This drove Felipe wild. The pleasure he got when he slipped his hand under her skirt and felt her naked skin ignited him with passion.

There was no doubt that Lucia learned more from her grandfather than she ever did at school. John Brown's laboratory was irresistible to a curious girl like her. She spent long hours in the lab, asking questions, getting answers, and conducting experiments. From her grandfather she learned—among many other things—to make matches, and to light them. Soon her parents forbade her from playing with matches at her house, because she almost burned a chair.

"I'm sure the matches you used to try to light that candle were very short, right?" said her sympathetic grandfather. "That's how they make them now. It probably lit so quickly that the fire reached your fingers before you could light the candle, and that made you drop the match on the chair."

"Were you watching me, Grandpa?" asked an astonished Lucia.

Chapter 6

"No," John chuckled, "But I can picture it clearly. Don't you worry, I'm going to teach you how to make long matches now, so you don't go burning your fingers, or burning down the ranch."

That day, while they made the matches, John told Lucia that every problem you can encounter in life has a solution. There's no problem or limitation that doesn't have an escape route if you use your imagination. Her grandfather explained this in context of the long matches, and it made perfect sense to her in the moment, but many years had to pass for Lucia to completely grasp the concept of imagination as a door that can free us from the prison imposed by our bodies, and that just as every night when we dream, we can leave our bodies every time we use our imagination. And most importantly, by leaving our bodies and interacting within an infinite field of possibilities through our mental and genetic memories, we transform.

When the matches were ready, Grandpa John put them in a silver matchbox that had the name Tita name engraved on it, and gave it to Lucia. The child loved the box, but was worried about its owner wanting it back one day.

"But Grandpa, this box isn't mine, it says Tita on it..."

"Yes, but I'm sure she would've loved for you to have it," he answered.

"Okay. But who's Tita?"

"She was your great-aunt, but she died before you were born."

Despite her young age, Lucia perceived that the box held a special meaning for her grandfather. She never could have imagined that he himself had made it, to give to Tita before their wedding. Lucia received the present with great respect and promised to take good care of it. To this date, she used the same tin matchbox to keep the matches she used to light the candles in the dark room every day. After bestowing the matchbox on her, Lucia's grandfather named her the family's Guardian of the Fire. Lucia accepted her new role solemnly and promised to herself that she would always make sure there was a fire in her home. That night, before she went to sleep, Lucia also decided she wanted to become a great alchemist when she grew up. She didn't even know the meaning of the word, but she'd heard her grandfather say it so she decided it must be important.

Lucia did eventually become a renowned chemist. But as the years passed, she became certain that the truest form of alchemy is love. Love light fires in our hearts. Love illuminates our thoughts. Love is what keeps those who have left us alive. We are the combination of our memories, in repetition and affirmation. But that doesn't mean it's eternal. Even genes change. Inside the human body, atoms and cells aren't always organized in one single predetermined manner. They can form new connections depending on a person's thoughts and emotions. That was Lucia's main concern, ever since she had created the Felipe of her dreams, night after night. He was real. He lived, breathed, danced, sang, and loved. What would become of him when she died? What happens to the ideal man when the person who dreams of him ceases to exist? Will he disappear along with her, or will he shine on, like the stars that still shine down on us even after their death? The Felipe of her dreams was as real, or even more so, as Felipe had been before his death. He was just a dream, yet "so what?" Lucia thought. Maybe we are all the dreams of a dream. In the end, the genetic chain that gives physical form to the person we fall in love with, is the product of someone's dream of permanence. In her case, the Felipe that visited her in dreams was incredibly real despite having disappeared many years before. Of his body nothing remained, it had been burned away when his body was cremated. Lucia and only Lucia kept him alive. She was the great alchemist that transformed her beloved Felipe's glowing presence into gold.

The only thing Lucia truly regretted was that the Felipe of her dreams had become so real, that the flesh-and-bones Felipe began to suspect that she was cheating on him with another man. His suspicions had begun one night, when Lucia was reaching an orgasm while facing the wall. It was so intense that she woke Felipe up. He took Lucia by the chin to look in her eyes and discovered she wasn't there. Her eyes betrayed the fact that she was somewhere else, light years from that bedroom. In that moment he thought Lucia was reaching ecstasy with someone else, thinking of someone else, which meant she must love someone else. Lucia was never able to explain to Felipe that one can be in two places at the same time and still be loving the same person. She also was unable to convince him that she had always remained faithful. From that day on, Felipe was unable to keep the jealousy at bay, and his insecurities began eating away at him slowly. He began to feel insufficient, not man enough for his wife. He began to drink heavily. His life collapsed, and so did Lucia's.

One of the worst moments in their life as a couple was the time their daughter Luz Maria overheard them fighting, and heard Felipe refer to Lucia as the "town whore." From that day on, Luz Maria became convinced that her mother was cheating on her father. Lucia had no explanation for her daughter; the reproach in Luz Maria's eyes disarmed her completely.

After that incident, Lucia gave up on her wet dreams with Felipe. Guilt became the great usurper, and began to dominate her mind and her dreams. Not having the strength to face it, Lucia gave in to the guilt, letting it turn her dreams into nightmares. She only made one attempt to expel the guilt of having hurt Felipe and having ruined her relationship with her daughter from her mind, but she failed completely. Now, at her age, she didn't even want to try. Lucia wasn't really interested in erotic dreams anymore. She was terrified of having a heart attack, or even pulling a muscle from an orgasm, so she'd given up on making love with Felipe a long time ago. On that early morning, she blessed Maria and Horacio's singing and laughter for pulling her out of her nightmares. The moonlight, shining through her window, gleamed in her eyes and brought a smile to her lips.

Scan to listen to *Smile*

Chapter 7

The smell of comal-roasted tomatoes filled the kitchen. Horacio slept like an angel next to the stove. Maria's body showed a drastic change, her weight was dropping at a great speed. This was because of several factors; first, because she was breastfeeding, second, because she was finally eating healthy at the ranch, and third, because she had discovered that grinding corn on a metate burned a lot of calories. Proof of that were all the expensive contraptions sold on the television, where you kneeled and pushed a wheel back and forth with your hands to get a flat belly. One got the same exercise with the metate, just twice as effective. Maria tried to grind at least half a pound of corn every day. That morning, she took a break and decided to try to make flour tortillas from scratch for the first time. She found it to be utterly sensual. It felt quite pleasurable to plunge her hands into the dough and knead it until the mix of flour and water was uniform. At the beginning of the session, when Lucia let warm water fall on the mound of flour and asked Maria to mix the ingredients, the young woman felt uncomfortable because of the way the dough stuck to her hands. But as she continued kneading, she found the act became something that could even be referred to as erotic. Feeling her fingers sink into the soft dough, caressing, compressing and molding, then letting the dough rest under a damp cloth before flattening it with a rolling pin was a wonderful way to channel her anxiety. The entire process, from mixing the lard with the flour, to turning it into a silky dough, was a relief during those days of reflection and anticipation. Just like Maria, the dough had to wait for the right time to expand, lengthen, broaden and then pass through purifying fire.

Lucia swelled with pride as she watched her granddaughter. Maria was a testament to the idea that blood carries information. Her hands reminded Lucia of her own mother Esperanza's, and just like Esperanza, Maria was acquiring cooking abilities at an alarming speed. She didn't need to hear instructions repeatedly, she seemed to be remembering the recipes as Lucia talked her through them. "Genes are genes" Lucia thought to herself, because that day Maria was less open to verbal communication. The young woman had a lot to sort out in her mind. The month she'd given Carlos had flown by, and it had not been nearly enough time to clarify her feelings. Each day came right after the other, like the paw of a feline after its prey, and just like the vote recount that was happening in the special election for governor of the State of Chihuahua. But unlike the world of politics—where it was obvious who the real winner had been, despite the system using all of its tricks to deny it, including buying votes shamelessly and manipulating information—nothing was clear in Maria's heart as she debated between the two candidates who were vying to be her lifelong companion. The man she would have conversations with, dance with, bathe with, go shopping for fruits and flowers, see movies with…the man she would laugh with!

That morning both candidates had contacted her, despite their previous agreement. Maria read Carlos' email first, only because it was the first one in her inbox.

"Maria, you ask something impossible of me: to keep quiet, to not contact you, to sit in a chair and wait patiently. I'm sorry, but I can't. I need to find a way to communicate with you somehow, to beg your forgiveness a thousand times over. I've tried to distract myself with literature, but every word I read makes me think of you. I've always been surprised by the banality of love. Everyone who's ever loved has felt the same way. It's amazing how someone who lived in Toledo in the 16th Century, a poet from the Middle Ages, or a bolero singer can describe parts of me that I never knew. That these people who never saw their reflection in your eyes, that never melted into your thighs, that never read the books we read together, nevertheless capture my emotions and remind me of words long forgotten that touch my soul. How could these people have felt about you the same way I do? How could they have so exquisitely described the sorrow your absence causes me? How could they have felt the delight of touching you, the pleasure of seeing you smile, the profound pain I experience from knowing that I caused the infinite sadness reflected in your eyes? I can't stop thinking about you, and of the day I can welcome you and my beloved Horacio back home. It seems as if my life is defined by hope and despair. I've become the character in a pastoral poem, complaining about your absence and counting the days until the time you requested of me has passed."

Maria was moved by the email. It was well written, but as usual Carlos spoke about himself, about his suffering and his pain. It was clearly the work of the literature professor who had seduced her precisely through poems and shared literary tastes. Sadly, that wise professor had to wait until he had "proof" before he accepted his own son, before he held him in his arms. He wasn't capable of loving Horacio until he was sure of his paternity.

Roberto's email was exactly the opposite:

"This morning, when I arrived at the hospital, I rode the same elevator where we first met. Now I know that you were going through a tremendous emotional crisis, yet you still smiled so warmly and kindly at me. I'm convinced that I fell in love with you that instant. You might think this affirmation is ridiculously forward due to the short time we've known each other, but it is what it is. And I wonder why I feel like I've known you forever, like my life had no substance before I met you. The only answer I can think of is that our encounter was predestined by something bigger than genetics, biology, or physics. That's the only explanation for the way you took my hand and allowed your body to melt with mine. It was as if love itself nudged you into my arms with the intention of finding a vessel in us. That was also evident when I ran into you and Horacio in the hallway on the fifth floor. I don't know how to explain this, but I can assure you there was something about your child that felt truly mine. Like he belonged to me, like he was asking me to see him grow and enjoy his enormous light. Maria, I don't want to distract you from the tremendous decision you have to make, but I feel the obligation to tell you that you should consider me ready to stand by your side, to enjoy the moments when my heart skips a beat, when my voice becomes hoarse, when my passion reaches you and we cry with joy. You are my fairy, my enchantment, I want to be with you in beaches, gardens, meadows, in rivers, while Horacio runs freely chasing after doves. I want you to know that no matter your decision, you'll forever be by my side. I will see you in everything that's beautiful, and I will hear your warm voice on cold winter nights. I will be the secret lover that awaits in the lyrics of your favorite songs, inviting you to dance until dawn. I am yours now and forever. You have a place in my soul that no one could ever take, it's here for you whenever you're ready."

In comparing the two letters, Maria came to the conclusion that while Carlos loved her, it was under certain conditions. Not Roberto, his love was unconditional. Roberto extended his love to her and Horacio with ease. Maybe the difference was that Roberto loved himself, and Carlos didn't. Carlos was a reserved, melancholy man who seldom trusted others, let alone showed affection. Roberto hugged without fear and without the expectation of anything in return. He was free of prejudice. The long nights that Maria had stayed up late she'd had enough time to think about her decision, but she wasn't certain of it yet. Where does the choice come from? How many other people were struggling with similar decisions? Maria shared genes with family members she never met, which meant she also shared their wrong conceptions, their paralyzing fears. She was convinced that guilty minds tend to seek out their own punishment. How many Mama Elenas were influencing her decision from the past? How many Titas invited her to rebel? How many Gertrudis gave her courage, and how many Rosauras pushed her to resign, and settle for her husband for the good of their child? Maria's responsibility was not only to herself and to Horacio, but to all the women in her family who made the wrong choices, who lived lonely and bitter lives because they thought the people they loved were forbidden or unattainable.

Carlos was one of those people who seem to accept those who break with societal conventions but condemns them deep down. She was sure that he would always consider their child the result of forbidden affairs of the past, of sinful liaisons that caused pain. And despite him saying he wanted to receive Horacio with open arms, Maria knew he never would. He had judged her so harshly on the color of their son's skin, that Maria knew that if went back to him he'd constantly find any excuse to condemn her. A leak, no food in the fridge, not paying the electric bill…any reason would suffice. Maria doubted that if she went back to Carlos things would go back to how they were before, but she still didn't have the courage to throw their relationship away.

"You know what, Grandma? I think I'm gonna start packing for my return to Mexico City…I have to get back to work."

"You plan on going to go back to work?"

"Yeah, I have no other choice, especially now that I'll be single."

"And you're not going to breastfeed your child anymore?"

"Well…I'll find a way to pump and leave him bottles of my milk…"

"And who will feed them to him?"

"Blanca, Fernando's wife. She's never had kids, and is willing to help me."

"Well, it seems like you've got it figured out. But there are other ways to solve…"

Maria interrupted: "I don't have many other options, Grandma. I either take up Blanca's offer or put Horacio in daycare."

Lucia took a deep breath before she replied. Like that morning that seemed so long ago now, when she explained to her granddaughter the benefits of sprouts, she spoke with great wisdom and care about her opinion on women's role in the present day.

"Maria, I think that you should give yourself more time. Don't go back to work so soon. When you're an old woman like me, you'll understand why."

"But Grandma…"

"Let me finish Maria. Then you can say anything you want. You're at crucial moment in your life and you need to take a breath. Don't feel pressured by duty, be it economic, social, family or professional. The world will always make you feel like you have something urgent to do, something to accomplish. But life can pass you by completely if you spend it trying to please everyone, because you're so afraid of disapproval. Take a pause, and do nothing for a while. It's like the silence between notes that makes a melody worth listening to. Your priority right now is to give yourself the time to make the right decision, because Horacio's future is at stake…"

"That's exactly why I have to go back to work!" Maria interrupted again. "How will I support him otherwise?"

"Are you going to let me finish, or not?" Lucia said sternly.

"Yes, Grandma. Sorry."

"Do you want to know why you eat compulsively? And I don't mean just you, but everyone who does. It's because we're a society that was weaned far too soon! We are a society forever in search of colostrum, so we substitute it with trans fats! But it doesn't matter how many potato chips you eat, they won't make up for the tit that you lost…Breastfeeding your child is the best thing you can do for now. He will grow up quickly, you'll see, and you won't regret having done it. What good is money in your hands if it doesn't give you the time to share the most intimate and sacred bond with your son, through which you pass on the collected knowledge of humanity?"

Maria had no words to answer with. Lucia went on.

"Let me tell you a story. When your grandfather became paralyzed, I was forced to go out and find a job. Neither of us had even considered it when we got married. Well, I looked for a job, and fortunately I found one easily. That wasn't the problem. I, along with many other women during World War 2, joined the labor force. The world's industrialization was blooming and we thought it was the best thing that could happen. We were wrong. We only have to look at the world we live in to realize it.

"I should've thought of another way, but I didn't. Now I know there's always another option. Always! Behind every woman who goes out in search of work there is a yearning, a dream. It's not that working is bad, it's the reason why that can be bad. We bet on the wrong dream, the one of modernity, progress, accumulation of wealth, mass production and industrialization. And it would have been worth it if we'd seen results in a collective well-being. But it wasn't the case…the dream of personal wealth is profoundly individualistic. It separates us from everyone and everything, including the environment. This leads to predation, to misery and ecological disasters. We forgot that dreams are ideas, images, thoughts that can shape matter for better or worse. When dreams are incorrectly focused, they become nightmares, like in the world of politics. It's clear how electoral institutions, congress and government no longer work. It's because the dream of riches has clouded everyone's minds. Corruption runs rampant. Money can buy anything, and is valued above all. If you ask people what they need to live, they'll answer: money. But that's false. What we need, first of all, is to eat. When people no longer have anything to eat, they'll start dreaming of food, they'll value the products that the Earth once dreamt of for all of us, because believe me, the Earth also dreams. Proof of this are flowers, corn, beans, squash, the millions of seeds that are slowly dying out, yet still she dreams and resists and waits for us to join her dream of planting, harvesting, sharing…We dream to forget the rules of an absurd world, to feel that the stars are with us even during the day, that's why it's important to stay with people who share your dreams, not your fears. Dreams of loving, or of breastfeeding. You say you want to return to Mexico City because you need to make a new home for yourself. I think that's fine, but first allow yourself to dream. Dreams are fertile soil."

And then Chencha burst into the kitchen with her smartphone in her hands to show them a video from the quinceañera of her granddaughter, who danced her first dance to Frank Sinatra's "The Impossible Dream." Lucia smiled. She couldn't have asked for a better song to emphasize her message to Maria. She had said her piece, and it was time to return to silence.

Scan to listen to *The Impossible Dream*

CHAPTER 8

The last few months had taken a toll on Lucia's health. A combination of factors that added up, beginning with the death of her daughter, the trip to Mexico City, the long nights trying to get her grandson Horacio to sleep, then the spirited dancing at Annie's party, and finally Carlos' unexpected visit to the ranch which had caused her back to act up.

Lucia decided to take a bath with mustard powder to relax her muscles. The problem was that she couldn't get in and out of the tub without assistance. Maria offered to help, and was pleasantly surprised at the incredible state of her grandmother's naked body.

"Damn, grandma, you don't have any cellulite!"

"Why is that strange? Am I supposed to?"

"No, well, it's just that every woman I know has some, even if just a little…"

"They must eat a lot of junk…"

"No grandma, not all of them. I have some friends that always watch what they eat, and they still have a lot of it."

"Hmm, but I'm sure they eat beef and chicken that's been fattened with hormones."

"Oh", Maria replied, taking a second to think. "I guess you're right."

"I can assure you that's the case! And I could also bet that your friends eat to fill a hole inside of them instead of for nourishment, and they ignore the fact that to eat is to have a dialogue with the universe. The figure you'll have depends on who you want to talk to, and about what.

As she listened, Maria lowered her grandmother into the bathtub with great care. Lucia was hanging from her granddaughter's neck, and both women felt relieved that Lucia wasn't overweight. Slowly and delicately, Maria lowered her grandmother into the warm water, and Lucia sighed with relief.

"Oh, that's nice."

"Well, Grandma, I'm sure you'll want to enjoy your bath, so I'll leave you to it. I'll be right outside. If you need something just call," Maria said hastily. She was in a hurry to check her cellphone. She'd felt the distinctive vibration of a text message and assumed it was from Roberto. But before she left the room, her grandmother's croaking voice stopped her:

"Please don't leave me alone."

Maria was shocked by the plea. It was the first time her grandmother had shown any sign of weakness. There was an almost imperceptible hint of fear in Lucia's voice, that didn't belong to the elderly woman herself. It had had snuck into her throat a long time before, when Felipe had begged using the same words in that very bathtub.

"Please don't leave me alone!"

"But that's what you want Felipe," Lucia had shot back bitterly, "to be completely alone. Stop tormenting me, I'm begging you! I've never cheated on you! When will you get that into your big, fat head?"

Felipe had been sitting in the tub while Lucia bathed and shaved him, which was quite a feat given her husband's ample facial hair. It was hard to give him a smooth shave without cutting him, because he had a lot of ingrown hairs in the neck area. Lucia had put a hot towel on his face to help open his pores.

It was Christmas morning. The previous night, Luz Maria and her children had gone back to their apartment before dinner due to the terrible fight caused by the argument over the Christmas presents. Felipe, as usual, had gotten plastered and had ruined the rest of the night. He'd woken up terribly hung over, had thrown up all over himself, and then demanded that Lucia bathe him.

"How many times did you fuck him, you slut?"

Lucia didn't answer. She was used to ignoring his aggressions. It wasn't the real Felipe who attacked her, it was a pathetic drunk who only came into their lives when Felipe drank. The Felipe she fell in love with had been the most delicate and decent man she'd ever known. So Lucia refused to speak to the devil, refused to acknowledge him.

"I'm talking to you! Answer me! How many times have you fucked him? Is he as big as me?" Felipe chuckled pathetically. "Or as big as I used to be? Tell me!"

In the face of Lucia's infuriating silence, Felipe took the hot towel off his face and in a swift motion wrapped it around his wife's throat with the intention of strangling her. Felipe had always been very strong, but now that he had been wheelchair bound, his arm muscles had developed even more. Lucia tried to escape to no avail, but finally was able to take a few steps back and out of Felipe's reach.

It took them both a few moments to recover from the physical exertion. Then Felipe reached for the table next to the bathtub where Lucia had placed all the tools she used to bathe and shave him and grabbed a pair scissors. He held the sharp tip right on his heart and shouted:

"I'm gonna kill myself. Watch me do it! That's what you want, right? For me to be gone so you can be free to fuck him…"

Lucia answered slowly, carefully weighing every word.

"You know what? I'm done. Congratulations, Felipe. You've reached my limit. I don't want to see you suffer anymore. I can't stand you playing the victim. You could still play the piano, sing on the radio. You have your amazing voice…you have me, you asshole! You've always had me, and I've always been faithful, but you never wanted to believe me, so…this is my limit. If you want to kill yourself, go ahead. I think it will be for the best…"

Lucia turned around and left the bathroom. She took a few minutes to recover and breathe deeply before she went back in. She couldn't leave Felipe in the tub, he wasn't capable of getting out on his own. The water must be cold by then. When she opened the door, she found her husband with his veins slit open, but still alive. Lucia ran to his side and took him by the face with both hands.

"Felipe, what have you done?"

Before Lucia was able to shout out for help, Felipe said softly:

"Don't call anyone. Just let me go…this isn't the life we dreamed of…"

Lucia and Felipe looked into each other's eyes for what seemed like an eternity, until Lucia saw that there was no one behind those blue eyes. A soft whisper was the last thing that came from Felipe's lips. Lucia kissed his face and his blood-soaked hands, those same hands that had caressed her countless times, that slid with grace and virtuosity over the piano keys. After a few minutes of this she called for help.

Chapter 8

The announcement of Felipe's passing came as a shock to everyone. When Luz Maria arrived at her parent's house, she blew up at her mother:

"You killed him! Murderer!"

Chencha had to step in before Luz Maria struck Lucia.

"Stop it child, your mother didn't..."

"She didn't what, Chencha?" Lucia screamed, tears rolling down her face. "How does a paraplegic get in the tub by himself and slit his wrists?"

Lucia had nothing to say. Her daughter was right, she was responsible for what had happened. She never should have left him alone, or told him to kill himself. For the rest of her life, Lucia considered herself a murderer. That was definitely the worst Christmas of their lives, and the winter cold settled in her family's hearts forever.

Just as water freezes in pipes during winter, the tears froze in in Lucia's tear ducts. She never cried over Felipe's death, not once did she spill liquid sorrow. It wasn't until that day, many years later, when she came face to face with her husband once again in the reflection of her bathwater, that she was able to cry the tears she'd held back for so long.

"I'll stay here with you Grandma, don't worry. What's wrong? Aren't you feeling well? Is it your hip?"

"No..." Lucia couldn't find the words to tell her granddaughter why she was weeping. And even if she could, she would find it hard to stop sobbing long enough to speak coherently. Maria remembered reading in Tita's diary how the author had been born amidst a river of tears.

"Grandma, do you want me to call the doctor?"

"No…listen…remember that we left a conversation unfinished?" Lucia asked, after calming down a little.

"What are you talking about?"

"About my infidelity."

"Oh. Yeah. But we don't need to talk about that right now…"

"We do!" interrupted Lucia. "This is the time."

A torrent of words erupted from Lucia's mouth, crawling over each other, weaving universes, neural connections, and lost memories as they materialized into sound waves that reached Maria's ears. Maria remained silent and didn't interrupt while Lucia talked, cried, cried and talked, making her confessions, until her final words:

"In vain do we hope to forget…"

Maria took her grandmother in her arms and kissed her forehead.

"Now I'd like to be alone," Lucia said.

"Ok Grandma, I'll give you a minute. Remember, I'm right outside if you need me."

Lucia wanted to be alone so she could close her eyes and enjoy Felipe, who was now back at her side. As soon as her eyes had liberated all the pent-up tears and allowed her to leave behind the guilt and pain, Felipe reappeared in her mind's eye. The Felipe of the first day they met, her eternal Felipe, the one she met at a party and who took her by the hand, showed her how to love. There he was again, tap dancing in his tailcoat suit and fine patent leather shoes to the rhythm of "The Best is Yet to Come."

Scan to listen to *The Best is Yet to Come*

Felipe opened his arms wide, inviting Lucia to dance with him. Lucia smiled widely, rose from the bathtub, and slid gracefully to the dance floor. The first thing she noticed was that her hip didn't hurt one bit, and that she was suddenly wearing a beautiful cocktail dress. As she approached Felipe she recognized the characteristic smell of his favorite cologne.

"That's strange," thought Lucia, "there's no sense of smell in dreams. That must mean this is real. I'm not imagining this, I'm really dancing with Felipe!"

Convinced of this, she decided she didn't want to wake up. What was the point? She stayed with Felipe.

When Maria came back into the dark room, she discovered her grandmother's lifeless body in the empty bathtub. Lucia had drained the bath before she closed her eyes. Her life energy had gone down the drain with the bathwater.

Maria was in shock. She remained silent, paying her respects as the last song from her grandmother's bath time playlist finished playing.

Chapter 9

Maria was breastfeeding Horacio, sitting on what used to be her grandmother's rocking chair. She felt a strange comfort in sitting in Lucia's spot, where her grandmother had once perhaps breastfed Luz Maria, Maria's mother. She was trying her hardest not to transmit to her son the profound sadness in her heart, but she wasn't sure she was succeeding. The boy, like her, was solemnly silent.

Maria felt cheated out of time with her grandmother, like a tamal that's removed from the pot before it's done cooking, like lovers distanced by death, like an under-exposed photograph. It was probably how Horacio felt when he drank from one of her breasts but wasn't satisfied, so he had to drink from the other. But unlike her child, she had no other resource to quell her thirst. Her grandma had left just when the stream of information between them was the strongest, when the Universe had connected their hearts and allowed all the possible knowledge to flow through their veins. Maria felt she needed more time to decipher and assimilate the ancestral knowledge that her grandmother transmitted every time she opened her mouth. In other words, she still needed time to heal the generational breach within her family caused by the rift between her mom and grandma, despite having imbibed knowledge, wisdom, generosity, and love during every minute she spent with Lucia. She felt like she used to when she didn't have an internet connection: disconnected from her grandmother and the culinary secrets she could've revealed to her, the new knitting patterns she could've shown her, the old family stories she could've told her. Lucia left her with a lot of pending assignments: the trip in search of the colors of Oaxaca; the natural dye workshop using cochineal burgundy and indigo, lessons on hydroponics, sowing and harvesting, dancing, sewing, and tailoring.

It was also a shame that Lucia would never get to see Horacio take his first steps, or taste the salad they were planning to make once they harvested the purple basil, or be around to help Maria decorate her new house with Roberto.

When Maria had found Lucia's lifeless body in the tub, the first person she thought of calling was Roberto. In that moment she understood that he was the man she wanted to share everything with, from the most devastating sorrow to the most sublime pleasure. She knew he would be her relief, her pillar, her life partner. Roberto had taken it upon himself to handle all of the paperwork pertaining to Lucia's passing. He had issued the death certificate himself, and was now helping Chencha clothe Lucia so her corpse could be transferred to the funeral home where the vigil would take place before she was cremated.

As soon as Roberto had arrived at the ranch, he had hugged Maria tightly and that was enough for both of them to know that they had one another forever. They briefly discussed that he was willing to stay with her that night, as long as that was what she wanted. Of course, Maria accepted, and not just for that night, but for the rest of their nights on this earth. Roberto's presence proved to be a blessing in the following hours. He acted as her safety net. As a cardiologist, he knew that one of the hardest moments for a grieving family is when the dead person is removed from the home. From that point on, there's no turning back. They're gone from what used to be their world. And it hurts like hell.

Maria watched her grandmother being carried out of the dark room in a stretcher and she couldn't hold back her tears. She bade her farewell with a kiss on the forehead. Lucia's body was icy, and the cold penetrated Maria's lips. She sought shelter in the dark room, because it was still warm from the candles they had lit to heat up the bath, and it still smelled of the red carnations that Lucia placed in Grandpa Felipe's altar every day. Maria said her last goodbye to her grandmother from the threshold. Lucia took with her all the presences that surrounded her, all her memories and dreams. The dreams seemed especially important at that moment.

Maria thought about her grandmother's dreams. It seemed unfair that dreams don't leave a footprint like genes do, despite also being information. It would be nice to be able to keep track of dreams. Maria wondered what the first black woman in her family dreamt of. No one would ever know, not even her name remained. All that was known of her was that she was the mother of Juan Treviño. He only kept that one photograph of her, with the name of the song "Strange Fruit" written in the back. Whoever wrote that must've done so after 1939, because that was when the song had first been recorded. She ruled out her grandfather Felipe, who would have been around nine years old. It must have been her great-grandfather Juan Felipe, who would have been 34, living in Chicago with Loretta Jackson, an exceptionally beautiful black woman. She imagined them sitting by their record player, listening to Billie Holiday's record and dreaming of a better future. Maria didn't think they could imagine having a great-great-grandson as handsome as Horacio in 2015, a child who had come to this earth to uncover secrets, to show what had been hidden. We always look for light in the dark, and that dark-skinned child shone brighter than anything or anyone. Or maybe she was wrong, and Horacio was the legacy of the desire of men and women who had dreamt the same thing generation after generation. Had Lucia ever dreamt of Horacio? She left before Maria could ask her that, and many other things. Now she had to find the answers on her own. She would have to tie up loose ends. Maria reflected upon the difference between a solitary thread and one that has been woven with others. She considered the difference to be abysmal; the thread that's alone lacks purpose, the one that's been woven is vast in significance. Maria felt like a lonely, disconnected thread. Just when she had found a member of her family that understood her and offered her unconditional support, she had been left alone again, and that made her feel terribly vulnerable. She thought that might be the reason why predators in the wild go after animals that have been separated from the pack, making them fragile. They don't dare attack a herd, they're not stupid or suicidal. Predators stalk until they find a small and distracted animal that gets separated from the herd to pounce on it...and Maria felt so far from her herd!

Out of the blue, an idea popped into her mind. Her grandmother hadn't left her as alone as she thought. There is a morphologic field where every thought or feeling an individual has can be shared with everyone else in an instant. The latest advances in science are leading us to the discovery of a universal spirit where every idea, every word, every action has an effect, and Maria was surrounded by presences, by whispers, by echoes, even if they eluded her senses. She never knew the genes that coursed through her veins until they manifested in Horacio, but they were there, waiting for the best moment to appear. And beyond those genes, there were the *rebozos*, the *huipiles*, the pots and pans, the *comales*, the knitting needles, the seeds, the trunk of memories, the photographs, the matches. Maria understood that information stays alive when we repeat it, when we share it, when we teach it to others. It's coded into every fabric, in every vase, in recipes, in the ceremony of sowing at the beginning of each season. When we recover our traditions, we recover our universal and cosmic origin. We recover our parents, our grandparents, and everything we thought we could have lost.

That was when Maria felt a hand on hers, which startled her and made her turn her head. She was surprised to see her sister Carolina, someone she'd thought she'd lost forever.

"Hey Maria. How are you?"

"What are you doing here?"

"What do you mean? I'm here for Grandma's funeral."

"I don't know if she would've wanted you here," said Maria, echoing the very words Carolina said the day that Lucia arrived at Luz Maria's funeral.

Carolina remained silent for what felt like an eternity.

"I know I haven't been the most supportive lately…" she began, only to be interrupted by Maria.

"Lately? Hmm."

"Especially with you…Horacio's birth stirred up old…"

"It didn't stir up shit! It brought blessings to this lousy family, and you should be grateful…"

"I am!" Carolina shouted. "Let me speak, please…it wasn't until you uploaded the pictures to Facebook that I remembered…"

"You're the oldest, Carolina. Are you really going to try to pretend that you didn't know your own grandfather was black?"

"I only remember his big blue eyes… everything else about him, I tried to forget…"

"Until your uncomfortable sister made you face everything you tried to evade."

"Yes, and for that I thank you. Forgive me… please forgive me Maria. I could barely hold it together after Mom's death, I just couldn't deal with anything…"

"Because you always put your pain before anyone else's."

"That's not true!"

"But it is! Do you think you're the only one who suffered over Mom's death? Didn't you stop to think how it could've affected me?"

"Oh my God, Maria, I've always thought of you! I've always tried to protect you, to keep you from suffering, from having to witness a violent death!"

"What do you mean? What violent death?"

"You clearly don't remember."

"Remember what?"

"The Christmas when Grandpa died."

"I don't remember but I know what happened. Grandma told me."

"I'm not talking about Grandpa's suicide. I'm talking about what happened afterwards."

"I have no idea what you're talking about."

Carolina took a deep breath and told her story as calmly as she could. Maria began to remember, little by little. Not everything, just enough to have a clearer idea of what had happened. Loose images began to materialize in her mind. Maria wasn't sure if they were real memories, or mental constructs from her sister's narration, but she began to hear her mother's hysteric screams and her father Ernesto's shouting, followed by the vision of her brother Fernando running out of the bathroom frantically, leaving a trail of bloody footsteps in his wake. Maria peeked into the bathroom to try to understand the uproar, and she saw her father trying to wrestle a knife away from her mother, a knife which she intended to use to kill Lucia. She thought she saw her grandmother sitting impassively, not even blinking in the face of grievous bodily harm or even death. Lucia was in a catatonic state. She wasn't crying, shouting, or even speaking. it was as if she'd lost the ability to see what was happening around her. Maria tried hard to remember more, but there was a big blank space in her memory. She managed to recall a moment when she made eye contact with her grandmother, whose eyes were shining with a powerful light. That was the last thing Maria saw, because Carolina took her by the hand and led her away from the bathroom. She took her to a bedroom and entertained her until she calmed down. For a long time Carolina held her little sister and stroked her hair, and told her Christmas stories to distract her. Because of that Maria was never aware that her mother had to be taken away to a mental institution to be treated for a nervous breakdown, and that her father had to get twenty-five stitches in his arm, the wound he got while trying to stop his wife from stabbing her own mother.

As her sister spoke, Maria began to relive a time in her life when Carolina had been very important to her. She could only half remember the years when her mom lived an absent and secluded life. After that tragic Christmas, her parents separated. Luz

Maria never agreed to sign divorce papers, and she lived the rest of her life ashamed of that winter morning. Carolina watched over her siblings. She took it upon herself to become the protector of the family, the one responsible for keeping her loved ones from seeing or hearing anything that might hurt them. She had to control everything, because she lived in constant fear of things getting out of hand. That was why, as soon as she learned of her grandmother's death, she took the first flight out to comfort and protect her baby sister.

"Now, please, tell me all about Grandma...You at least got her back before she died...I didn't...but first, give me a hug."

The two sisters embraced. Maria half-heartedly, but Carolina squeezed her with all her love. That allowed the heavens to open up, and Maria felt her mother, her two grandmothers, her four great-grandmothers, eight great-great-grandmothers, and so on until the dawn of mankind. It was the hug of all hugs. It was the embrace that Lucia never gave Luz Maria before they passed away. It was the embrace that got lost in time the day that some white men kidnapped "Strange Fruit's" grandfather off the coast of Africa. The embrace lingered in the arms of a desperate mother whose child was taken from her. She saw him being dragged away from the beach, and she raised her arms to the sky, praying to her gods to keep him safe. It was the sum of every desire to protect another. It was all that and more. After their hug, the two sisters were able to weep over their mother's and their grandmother's deaths.

Later in the day, Maria opened the trunk of memories for her sister, and she silently thanked Lucia for having kept a record of their family's past, not just for her, but for all of them. Maria was touched to see Carolina crying over the photographs that revealed a hidden past that she had refused to see for so many years.

That night, before she went to sleep, Carolina wrote in her diary:

"I look ahead and am blinded by the sun.

I look behind and I see that my body casts a shadow.

Wasn't I supposed to be the sun?

Didn't I shine enough to light others?

I'm overcome by sorrow.

I'm not who I thought I was.

I can't even reflect the light that my body receives, I just turn it into a shadow.

If I can't reflect the light, and therefore can't augment the presence of light,

it means I am nothing but an interference, a hindrance.

What if I give up on being myself?

What If I leave aside my desire to control?

Maybe I would simply become light."

The following day the two sisters went to the reading of Lucia's Will. Fernando was the last to arrive from Mexico City. The Will had been recently modified with a notary after the first week that Maria and Horacio arrived at the ranch.

"I, Lucia Brown-Múzquiz, of sound body and mind…leave my granddaughter Carolina Pérez Alejandrez all the money in my bank accounts. To my grandson Fernando Pérez Alejandrez I leave the house I own in Mexico City. To my granddaughter Maria Pérez Alejandrez I leave my trunk full of photographs and personal effects, as well as the fire-proof safe that's inside my closet. I also want her to have the following objects:

1) My comal.

2) My vinyl records.

3) My knitting needles.

4) The *molcajete* that Tita used to make the rose petal sauce for the first time.

5) The *metate* with which my grandmother Esperanza taught me to grind cacao.

6) My wrought iron pots and pans.

My eco-products company "Green Fumarole," as well as this ranch and everything in it, goes to my great-grandson Horacio Fuentes Pérez, to be managed by his guardian and mother Maria Pérez Alejandrez until he turns eighteen years of age."

Maria wept through the entire reading. She knew she was the luckiest of the three siblings. Her grandmother had left her her most prized possessions. Maria was not only honored, she was profoundly grateful. She felt gratitude for her mother, for her grandmother, for everyone and everything. She was sad that her mother had died thinking that Lucia was a murderer, because that had caused so much pain for the entire family. Pain and separation. Nonetheless, both women had done their part to restore what had been broken. Maria now knew that there's an invisible order that always leaves the door open to the possibility of peace, unity, and love. If Maria hadn't given birth to Horacio, and if her mother hadn't died because of the shock, Lucia wouldn't have taken Maria with her to the ranch, and the reparation of all harm done would've been impossible. Maria would never have learned to knit, to make flour tortillas, to find pleasure in culinary activities, and the meaning behind the small things we do in the intimacy of our homes. And under no circumstances would she have had an opportunity to become a teacher for her older sister. Carolina was mesmerized by the wisdom that her little sister distilled from her every pore. She was surprised by the amount of knowledge that Maria had acquired in the short period of time she spent with their grandmother. Carolina never imagined Maria would be able to cook like this! The younger sister was making breakfast at the same time as she explained to Carolina how she'd lost so much weight with minimum effort.

"When you eat correctly, your body reacts immediately."

"I can tell! You look great."

"And I feel great! One of the things I learned, is that the health and well-being that can come from whatever you put in your mouth depends on the quality of information that's shared between your cells."

"Oh," Carolina said wistfully. "I'm jealous that I missed out on her teachings."

"Well, if you want, I can pass most of them along...It won't be exactly the same, but it'll be similar...did I tell you that she had no cellulite?"

"Get out of here!"

"Yeah, she told me that we eat so much crap, hell, they're even beginning to put plastic in processed food! Imagine that! Who knows what they add to sliced bread now that it never goes bad. And don't get me started on all the preservatives and chemicals they put in everything."

"I know, it's awful."

"Grandma once told me that eating is like having a conversation with the universe, and if we eat junk food or genetically modified food, it's more like we're having a conversation with a chemical lab…you get it, right? Those conversational partners lack nature's touch, and that's why they don't nourish. So then to fill that hole we feel, we go into this vicious cycle where we try to eat everything we can, but since our cells don't feel they're getting the right nutrients, we keep eating and storing fat until we're like pigs."

"Interesting. Hey, by the way, you never went back to the therapist I recommended, did you?"

"That was you?" Maria asked, looking up from her chopping and frying and tortilla rolling for the first time.

"Yeah, why?"

"Damn, Carolina, I should've known it was you! Thank God I didn't find out until now, otherwise I would've insulted you even worse."

"Why?"

"Because she was a total bitch…"

Carolina and Maria burst out laughing at the same time. They talked and talked, trying to make up for all the lost years, happy to have found each other again. Their voices sounded excited and euphoric as the words just kept pouring out. After breakfast they got dressed so they could go the funeral home for their grandma's cremation. The only moment they stopped talking was when Lucia's body met the fire, which received her with all the honor befitting such a grand woman. The flames licked strongly, with passion. The two sisters. arm in arm, saw the Guardian of the Fire go up in flames. The tears in their eyes made them miss a firefly that emerged from the flames and rose toward the sky.

Back in the waiting room, they resumed their conversation. Maria told Carolina her conclusions about their family history. Now it was very clear to her why she didn't like Christmas. As for Carolina, she confessed that she finally understood Horacio's birth as a blessing for the family. He was a beautiful boy who was destined to reunite and heal. The two sisters made a series of connections, of signs, songs, and words that they had missed or that had remained unseen, but that held within them the destiny of their family, as in the case of John Brown, whose last name had predicted the color of Horacio–his great-great-great grandson's skin.

When the cremation was over, everyone headed back to the ranch. Maria, Carolina, Fernando, Horacio, Roberto, and Chencha. Together they held an intimate ceremony which consisted of lighting the candles of the dark room with the matches they took from the silver box John had made for Tita. They sat and listened to Lucia's favorite records. At dawn, when Horacio's bawling announced the new day, they took Lucia's ashes and mixed them with Felipe's in a single urn, which they then emptied in the Rio Grande. The ashes were the same color.

That night, after putting Horacio down and joining Roberto in bed, Maria opened the fireproof safe in Lucia's closet. It wasn't easy. First, she had to fight the overwhelming nostalgia she felt from smelling her grandmother's characteristic smell, which had impregnated all the clothing. Then she had to get over the feeling of being an intruder who had no right to rifle through her grandmother's personal belongings. And finally, she was able to confront a past full of magic and alchemy.

The first thing she found in the safe was a locket that had pictures of José Treviño and Mama Elena. Then, a velvet box containing the pen and penholder that Tita had used to write in her diary. She also recognized a pair of glasses and a pair of cufflinks that must've belonged to John Brown. Maria had never seen these objects before, probably because they held such a special meaning for her grandmother. And in the back of the safe, Maria found a small cardboard box that was tied to an envelope with a small silk bow. Inside the box were firefly wings, so many firefly wings. The envelope contained a letter that her grandmother had written before her death.

"Dear Maria, if you're reading this letter, then I'm no longer alive. These firefly wings are one of my most prized possessions. My mother left them to me when she died. She caught the fireflies the day that Grandpa John married Shirley, and put them under her dress so they illuminated her body right near her heart. In that shining moment, and despite her young age, she swore to herself she would marry Alex, my father. That's why I was named Lucia, in honor of that beautiful, bright sunset.

I named my daughter Luz Maria for a similar reason, because I felt deep inside the desire for her to be born with that same joy, that same light. Then she named you Maria, just Maria, with no light before. I don't know her reasons for that, but now I want to name you the Guardian of the Fire, the position bestowed upon me by my grandfather in my youth. You are the right person for the responsibility. You were able to show us what we tried to hide, what we tried to not see. Fortunately, light is impossible to hide, it will always leave a trace: a shadow, which will serve as a guide to discover where the light originates. When all we see is the shadow, we miss out on so much. Light manifests when someone dares to break open the curtains of darkness. You were that person, you gave birth to light, you know better than anyone how to see it, how to care for it, how to praise it. Thank you for everything Maria."

Chapter 10

The following Christmas was Maria's moment of truth. She had decided to cook Christmas dinner for all her family and friends. Truth be told, everyone had pretty low expectations considering she'd never cooked a meal like that in her life. Most people thought that even the months Maria had spent with Grandma Lucia wouldn't have been enough to get her ready to prepare a dinner for fifty people. But Maria had Chencha as a helper, and that was a guarantee that things would go well. Surprisingly, the only one who didn't doubt her was Carolina, since she'd already tasted Maria's cooking. She was so enthused that she offered to be an assistant, even though she wound up getting in the way more than she helped. But Maria appreciated the intention, and her sister's presence and small talk proved to be pleasant. A couple of times Carolina's desire to control bubbled to the surface, but Maria quickly put her in her place. Maria's relationship with her siblings had been greatly strengthened. Tita's diary had become a guide that allowed them to analyze the negative and destructive behaviors that had been present in their family for generations: the urge to control, the fear of emotional loss, the decision to obey submissively rather than face the guilt that comes with the transgression of rules, or the flip side of that coin: a strong rebellion against any form of authority. All three of them agreed that they wanted to find a way to be free from oppression. During their long conversations, Maria and her siblings also discussed at length the tragic chain of events that must have happened at a national level for Mexico to lose its wonderful culinary and herbal traditions.

They couldn't fathom how, despite Mexican Cuisine being an Intangible Cultural Heritage of Humanity, Mexico had the highest number of Diabetic and Overweight children per capita in the world. Little was left of the wisdom of those women who worked the fields in 1910, sowing, harvesting, feeding, fighting for social change. Where did we lose our way? Where did the thread become unraveled? How can we recover what we have lost?

Maria and Roberto had moved into the ranch, where they tended her garden and crops. Fernando and his wife Blanca tried to get together with Carolina for dinner at least once a week. They cooked, then ate together. Whenever either of them invented a new recipe, they would share it via email, with the intention of creating a new cookbook for the next generations. They also included natural recipes and home remedies that would help heal all kinds of ailments. Maria was the biggest contributor, because she had a gift for imagining new and nutritious recipes. That Christmas, for example, she was dead set on making Chiles in Nogada Sauce, but since it was December there were no walnuts or pomegranate, two key ingredients. Maria decided she would make a Thai sauce instead. In place of walnuts she used cashews, and mixed in some ginger, lemongrass, and coconut milk. As a substitute for pomegranate she used dried cranberries, and the result was spectacular. The Thai sauce enhanced the spiciness of the chiles, complementing the sweetness of the stuffing. Of course, Chencha almost dropped out several times. Maria was too creative for her, not heeding most of Chencha's warnings, breaking the rules constantly. But Chencha had to admit that everything went well and tasted delicious. The Christmas Rolls were one of the highlights of the night. Maria stuck to the traditional family recipe, having no objection about finely mincing the onion.

Roberto was in charge of the night's musical playlist. Maria felt so blessed to have found this man. He loved music and was an excellent dancer. With Carlos, she'd never been able to enjoy parties. He would just sit all night, and if Maria forced him to dance with her, he'd do so halfheartedly, just swaying from side to side without the smallest hint of grace or sensuality. Roberto was overflowing with both, and in addition, Roberto and Maria shared the same musical tastes, perhaps because families tend to pass such things on to their children. And in a way the "Orchestra Wives" Annie and Lucia had transmitted their passion for certain artists and dance styles. Roberto could dance anything, from swing to ska, to rock and roll, salsa, and cumbia. That night he was playing music from Lucia's vinyl collection, and just as the song "At Last" began to sound, Maria appeared in the dining room with a large tray of Chiles in Thai Sauce. Roberto took the tray from her, put it down on the table, then took her by the wrist and danced with her as close as they could, considering Maria's large pregnant belly.

Scan to listen to *At Last*

Maria was now happily divorced thanks to the wonderful lawyer Carolina recommended. The battle was tough, because Carlos didn't want to sign the divorce papers and stalled as much as he could. He sued Maria for adultery, because she was living with Roberto. This turned out to be a great mistake, because the judge then conceded the divorce automatically. Maria was worried that Carlos might try to get full custody of Horacio, but that never happened. Carlos must have imagined his life as the single father of a black boy, and probably didn't like the idea.

Maria was, for the first time, enjoying a happy Christmas. Until the moment when everything almost collapsed because Horacio, who was now crawling all over the house like a tiny hurricane and was even taking his first steps, took advantage of the distraction to cause mischief. Chencha was the first one to notice:

"What is this child doing? Who's supposed to be looking after him?

Horacio was sitting on the living room floor with Tita's silver matchbox in one hand, and with the cardboard box of firefly wings in the other. He had found a way to open them and was happily chewing the contents of both. Maria was at fault for leaving the matchbox within the child's reach after she used the matches to light the candles in the dark room—part of her grandmother's daily ritual which Maria now continued—but no one could explain how Horacio had gotten his hands on the firefly wings.

"Nooo! Horacio, what are you doing?" Maria yelled. "Who the hell left the trunk of memories open?

Roberto ran towards the child and quickly got the matches and firefly wings out of his mouth. Horacio clung to Roberto's neck and wailed. His mother's yells had scared him. Maria walked over to her son, but she was bewildered. She stared into nothing for a second, as her memory took her to a remote past. Once again she was peeking inside the dark room as a child, and she saw her grandfather Felipe with his head leaning against the edge of the tub. His eyes were closed but his mouth was wide open. Maria was shocked by her grandfather's dead expression. Then she caught a glimpse of a small dot of light that seemed to come from within his throat, and suddenly a firefly flew out of his gaping mouth! Lucia noticed the insect as well, and looked around to see if anyone else had noticed. Maria locked eyes with her Grandma, who despite the terrible gravity of the situation, almost smiled. The firefly flew very close to Lucia's eyes and made them shine with a powerful light. That reflection was not lost on the young Maria, but at that moment a tug from her sister Carolina led her away from that place. Horacio's loud cries brought Maria back to the present. She began to stroke his back to calm him down.

From high above, in another dimension, Lucia was greatly enjoying the scene. She had been present all day, in case her granddaughter needed her. She was at Maria's side while she prepared the banquet, approving of the way Maria set the table, of how she decorated the house, and of how she recreated the recipe for Chiles in Nogada. Maria had only one thing left to learn, and that was the recipe for the ceremonial chocolate, and the song that must accompany the drinking of it to achieve the desired effect. After that night, Lucia had no doubt that Maria would find this on her own. Next to Lucia, as always, was Felipe, who at that moment was quietly—almost in a whisper—singing in his great-grandson's ear a lullaby that his mother Loretta had sung to him every time she tried to get him to sleep. The boy responded in-stantly, ceased his crying, and floated off into the dreamworld. There, all his relatives awaited him.

Scan to listen *When the Saints Come Marching In*

Chapter 10

And once more, like in a Broadway musical, "When the Saints Come Marching In" began to play loudly, and everyone sang along to the words: Tita, Pedro, Mama Elena, José Treviño, Nacha, John, Shirley, Gertrudis, Juan, Chencha, Rosaura, Alex, Esperanza, Juan Felipe, Loretta, and Morning Light. They all marched down a street in New Orleans following Louis Armstrong's beat. The marching band was headed by Lucia, Felipe, and Horacio—or Luciano—who was flying and singing louder than everyone else with his powerful firefly voice, a voice that was forever free.

"Oh when the Saints go marching in
When the Saints go marching in
O Lord, I want to be in that number
When the Saints go marching in"

The boy responded instantly, ceased his crying, and floated off into the dreamworld. There, all his relatives awaited him. And then, as happens only in Broadway musicals, "When the Saints Come Marching In" began to play, and the entire group was singing along to the words, joined by everyone who had once been part of their lives: Tita, Pedro, Mama Elena, José Treviño, Nacha, John, Shirley, Gertrudis, Juan, Chancha, Rosaura, Alex, Esperanza, Juan Felipe, Loretta, and Morning Light.

"Oh when the Saints go marching in
When the Saints go marching in
O Lord, I want to be in that number
When the Saints go marching in"

Free now, forever free, they proceeded down a street in New Orleans to the beat of Louis Armstrong, led by Lucia, Felipe, and Horacio, who was almost flying as he sang louder than the whole chorus with his powerful firefly voice.

Music Credits

On the Sunny Side of the Street: Composed by Jimmy McHugh;
Lyrics by Dorothy Fields
    Vocals: Leika Mochán
    Organ: Nicolás Santella
    Bass: Israel Cupich
    Drums: Gustavo Nandayapa
    Guitar: Demián Gálvez

Where or when: Composed by Richard Rodgers; Lyrics by Lorenz
Hart
    Vocals: Fernando Ruiz-Velazco
    Piano: Nicolás Santella
    Bass: Israel Cupich
    Drums: Gustavo Nandayapa
    Guitar: Demián Gálvez
    Saxophone: Daniel Zlotnik
    Trumpet: Jerzain Vargas

I'll Be Seeing You: Music by Sammy Fain; Lyrics by Irving Kahal.
    Vocals: Sylvie Henry
    Piano and organ: Nicolás Santella
    Bass: Israel Cupich
    Drums: Gustavo Nandayapa
    Pedal steel guitar: Demián Gálvez

Some Enchanted Evening: Music by <u>Oscar Hammerstein II</u>; Lyrics by <u>Richard Rodgers</u>
  Vocals: Regina Orozco
  Piano: Nicolás Santella
  Bass: Israel Cupich
  Drums: Gustavo Nandayapa
  Pedal steel guitar: Demián Gálvez
  Flute: Daniel Zlotnik
  Trumpet: Jerzain Vargas

When You're Smiling: Written by Larry Shay, Mark Fisher and Joe Goodwin
  Vocals: Leika Mochán
  Piano: Nicolás Santella
  Bass: Israel Cupich
  Drums: Gustavo Nandayapa
  Guitar: Demián Gálvez
  Saxophone: Daniel Zlotnik
  Trumpet: Jerzain Vargas

Smile: Written by John Turner, Charles Chaplin, Geoffrey Parsons
  Vocals: Sylvie Henry
  Piano: Nicolás Santella
  Bass: Israel Cupich
  Drums: Gustavo Nandayapa

Music Credits

The Impossible Dream: Composed by Mitch Leigh; Lyrics written by Joe Darion

Vocals: Fernando Ruiz-Velazco

Piano and synthesizer: Nicolás Santella

Bass: Israel Cupich

Drums: Gustavo Nandayapa

Guitar: Demián Gálvez

Saxophone, flute: Daniel Zlotnik

Trumpet: Jerzain Vargas

The Best is Yet to Come: Composed by Cy Coleman; Lyrics by Carolyn Leigh

Vocals: Fernando Ruiz-Velazco

Piano: Nicolás Santella

Bass: Israel Cupich

Drums: Gustavo Nandayapa

Guitar: Demián Gálvez

Saxophone Daniel Zlotnik

Trumpet: Jerzain Vargas

At Last: Written by Mack Gordon and Harry Warren

Vocals: Regina Orozco

Piano and organ: Nicolás Santella

Bass: Israel Cupich

Drums: Gustavo Nandayapa

Guitar: Demián Gálvez

When the Saints Go Marching In
    Vocals, harmonica, guitar: Genaro Palacios Clemow
    Vocals and washboard: Genaro Palacios
    Bass: Pedro Durán

Recorded at Topetitud Estudios, Coyoacán, Mexico City, Fall 2019.
    Audio Engineer: David Montui
    Mixed and Mastered by: Ricardo Acasuso
    Produced and arranged by: Demián Gálvez
    Executive producer: Laura Esquivel.

About the Author

Laura Esquivel started out as a teacher and multi-awarded screenwriter. Her first novel, Like Water for Chocolate, has sold over 7 million copies worldwide and has been translated to more than 30 languages. Other books by her available in English are The Law of Love, Swift as Desire, Malinche, Pierced by the Sun, and Tita's Diary which along with this book rounds out the Like Water for Chocolate Trilogy.